JUST SIX GUESTS

If you want to know how...

Buying & Running a Guesthouse or Small Hotel
Make a fresh start and run your own guesthouse

Starting and Running a B&B
*A practical guide to setting up and managing
a Bed and Breakfast business*

Watching the Bottom Line
Financial management for small businesses

Cash Flows & Budgeting Made Easy
How to set and monitor financial targets in any organisation

howtobooks

Send for a free copy of the latest catalogue to:

How To Books
3 Newtec Place, Magdalen Road,
Oxford OX4 1RE, United Kingdom
email: info@howtobooks.co.uk
http://www.howtobooks.co.uk

HELEN JACKMAN

JUST SIX GUESTS

First-hand, encouraging advice
on how to set up and run
a small Bed & Breakfast

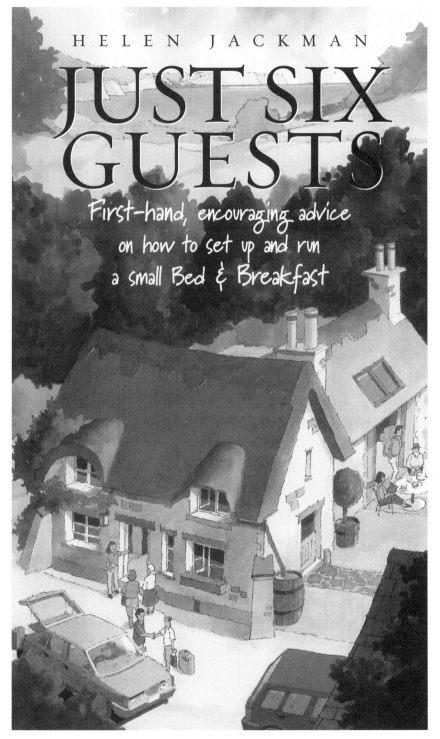

howtobooks

First published by How To Books Ltd,
3 Newtec Place, Magdalen Road,
Oxford OX4 1RE. United Kingdom.
Tel: (01865) 793806. Fax: (01865) 248780.
email: info@howtobooks.co.uk
www.howtobooks.co.uk

First published 2004

British Library Cataloguing in Publication Data
A catalogue record for this book is available from the British Library

Produced for How To Books by Deer Park Productions, Tavistock
Cover design by Baseline Arts Ltd, Oxford
Cover illustration by David Mostyn
Typeset by PDQ Typesetting, Newcastle-under-Lyme, Staffs.
Printed and bound in the UK by Bell & Bain Ltd, Glasgow

NOTE: The material contained in this book is set out in good faith for general guidance and no liability
can be accepted for loss or expense incurred as a result of relying in particular circumstances on
statements made in the book. The laws and regulations are complex and liable to change, and readers
should check the current position with the relevant authorities before making personal arrangements.

Contents

List of Illustrations

Preface

Seven years have passed since we welcomed the first strangers into our home, so I now feel qualified to comment on our experience and include information that we have found helpful. I am prompted to do so because, in advance of taking what seemed at the time quite a brave step, I could not find any British publication providing general guidance on this 'hobby' end of the market. The assumption, confirmed by newspaper articles, was that anyone can let a couple of spare rooms; but when one's home is being invaded it is essential to be aware of the requirements and potential problems if it is not to be a regretted experience.

We admit a prior interest. My husband spent all his working life in the hospitality industry and we first met whilst studying hotel and catering management at the same college back in the late 50s. My first work experience was during a summer vacation employed as a chambermaid, as they were then called, at the Redcliffe Hotel in Paignton – he was a waiter in the same hotel. Now, nominally retired, we have gone full circle – back to serving meals and making beds! We have a division of labour, following this pattern, which works well for us – my husband is responsible for everything relating to the dining room and I am responsible for the bedrooms. My load is lighter when visitors stay for several nights.

A POSITIVE EXPERIENCE

The difference between our early experience and the present is that we now fill our empty bedrooms with guests as a pleasure, rather than financial necessity, and having the world come to us has been a bonus. Not all operators would agree but we have found opening up our home to visitors has been a very positive experience, providing a reason for redecorating and putting more effort into the garden. We enjoy providing guests with a relaxing stay and like to think that we do our bit in improving international relations. Tolerance, flexibility and a sense of humour have been needed on occasions, but nearly all our guests have been great and since starting our business our faith in humanity has soared.

This has been our experience in rural Kent, where the main attractions are the castles, stately homes and gardens and our clientele generally reflect these interests. Others may have a different story to tell. Guests come from all walks of society and countries of the world, which means welcoming those with different customs and lifestyles into your home. We have hosted visitors from Japan, the Middle East, Australia and New Zealand, North and South America, South Africa, Scandinavia and most of the countries in Europe. They have arrived on foot, on bicycles and motorbikes, in clapped-out Fords and classic cars, Minis and Mercedes, white vans and builders' lorries. Some have turned up on our doorstep in designer wear with matching luggage; some in anoraks, muddy walking boots with back packs and yet others covered in tattoos and clutching sports bags. One can never be sure who will be coming over your threshold next but you can be assured that the mode of transport or trappings of affluence will have little bearing on the geniality or personal standards of your guests. If you find it difficult to trust, respect and enjoy others, or place a high value on the privacy of your own home, B&B is probably not for you. Not all providers enjoy the experience or make a success of it.

Although much of it is common sense I hope this book will answer a few questions and provide an insight into what can be expected from a small-scale operation, without appearing too patronising. And bear in mind we may not always practise what we preach!

Helen Jackman

Acknowledgements

This book has benefited enormously from the publications issued by VisitBritain and the regional and national Tourist Boards. The advice of our local Tourist Information Centre, Quality Assessment inspectors and owners of the B&Bs we have stayed in around the world has been much appreciated. Thanks are due to them, to Christine Sheppard for reading and commenting on the draft and Ted Finley for his practical contribution. Thanks are also due to my husband for donning an apron with enthusiasm and most of all to our guests who have given us the pleasure of their company and paid us for the privilege.

Introduction

A French family with two young daughters booked in for a few days. This was the girls' first visit to England and we were apparently the first English people they had ever spoken to – they were also on a very tight budget. We helped them plan their days in London and the Kent countryside and they showed us each morning the diary they were writing up of this special holiday. Their interest and enthusiasm for everything English gave us a real boost and is typical of the satisfaction we have derived from our hobby/business in the hospitality industry – we even forgave them for consuming two loaves at breakfast each day!

I describe it as a 'hobby' but there are also financial rewards. We can accommodate just four guests in two double rooms, currently at £50 per room per night (modest for our area). If we achieved 100% occupancy we would have a gross income of £700 per week and £36,400 a year; with the permitted statutory six guests in three rooms this could rise to £54,600. Regrettably we don't achieve this or anywhere near. Indeed I doubt if anybody would as national statistics indicate that 40% is a fair bed occupancy for serviced accommodation and depending on the locality some areas quote 30% as a more realistic estimate. Like most providers our business fluctuates, with very few guests between November and March. Even during times of the year when there are plenty of visitors looking for accommodation, with only two rooms we cannot be sufficiently flexible to keep both full. Without doubt the main motivation for the small operator has to be the enjoyment gained from sharing your home and the seasonal aspect can be a bonus for it allows you to take long holidays during the quiet months.

B&B AND THE TOURIST INDUSTRY

Bed and breakfast is a valuable sector of the British tourist industry. Despite a few setbacks it has grown to record levels in the past decade and has long since shed its image of the 'seaside landlady' with her curfews and dodgy cooking. With greater professionalism amongst providers it is less likely to be viewed as budget accommodation and is becoming quite fashionable amongst overseas tourists.

Since April 2003 those of us living in England, Wales, Scotland and Northern Ireland have come under the umbrella of VisitBritain (the result of a merger between the English Tourism Council and the British Tourist Authority) and our national and regional tourist boards (RTBs). VisitBritain is responsible for marketing Britain to overseas customers and encouraging the domestic market to take more and longer holidays at home. It is the VisitBritain website which is the source of most of the statistics in this book.

VisitBritain also supports a National Quality Assurance Standards scheme. Properties registered with the scheme are assessed against pre-established standards of excellence, with B&Bs in England being awarded diamonds and those in Scotland, Wales and Ireland receiving stars, graded from 1 to 5 according to quality. Currently there is no compulsion to participate in the inspection schemes to open up as a B&B except in Northern Ireland, where the Tourist Board inspects all accommodation providers annually, under a statutory system.

New providers will be warmly welcomed by their local Tourist Information Centres (TICs) as the source for first-hand information and, as an encouragement for the hobby provider, the 'six guests/ three bedrooms' concession, which excludes you from some of the red tape which applies to those offering more accommodation, has been set up. Of those advertising in our local guide under the 'Bed Breakfast and Guest House' section over 90% fall within this threshold.

The concession applies to England, Wales and Scotland but not Northern Ireland, though much of the general information regarding small operators applies across the whole of the British Isles. By sticking to this limit it is less likely that you will have to apply for planning permission, register with the fire authorities or pay business rates. However, as guests will be sleeping and eating in your home you will have a number of legal obligations – health and safety and public liability insurance come immediately to mind and others, though not mandatory, constitute good practice, so we have found it to our advantage to take the recommendations on board. The VisitBritain *Pink Booklet* is the definitive source for all statutory requirements.

OPENING UP YOUR HOME

If B&B is to be your sole source of income we would suggest you need at least six letting bedrooms. It is more realistic for those sticking within the 'six guests' concession to view it as an extra. We have found it a useful alternative to full-time employment whilst easing into retirement, whilst others appreciate the flexibility it gives if one partner wishes to work at home whilst the other has a full-time job, maybe because they still have a family to care for. Yet others, such as artists, writers and consultants have found it provides the social contact they miss because their main occupation is also carried on from their home.

Whatever your personal circumstances you will be opening up your home to the public and will need patience and flexibility as guests do not conform to regular schedules. They may arrive at any time between 10am and midnight and want breakfast at any time between 6.30 and 10am. For these reasons it might be difficult to operate if holding down a full-time job elsewhere.

If you have a suitable home, or the wherewithal to acquire one, B&B can be an appealing option for a small family-run business. To the casual observer letting a couple of rooms overnight is something anyone with a modicum of commonsense can turn his or her hands to. We all clean our homes, make beds, and anyone can knock up a fried breakfast; at £20/£30 per head per night this can look like a nice little earner, but the failure rate is surprisingly high. According to the *Which Guide to Working at Home*, one in four businesses gives up within three years. It would be a mistake to view it as easy money for doing very little and because of higher expectations amongst customers and competition within the sector there is now a much greater need for professionalism.

The emphasis in this book is on the small 'hobby' operator but much of the information will also relate to larger ventures.

Researching the Project

IS IT RIGHT FOR YOU?

Bed and breakfast provides an opportunity to start a business almost anywhere in the country at relatively low cost but any business venture, however low-key, needs pre-planning and research.

Is there a market for this sort of operation? Can you afford to do it? Will you enjoy the experience? Does your property, or the property you intend to buy, have suitable accommodation and is it in a location that is likely to attract customers? What type of venture do you have in mind – a traditional bed and breakfast providing a service in the locality where it is situated, or a luxury 'home hospitality' package where guests join the hosts for gourmet dinners in candlelit dining rooms? Paramount is an examination of your personal objectives, as all other decisions will depend on this.

TOURIST PATTERNS

If B&B providers are to get their fair share of the tourist traffic it is helpful if they understand the trends so they can focus on the right markets from the outset. Surveys,[1] carried out in 2002, show that tourism in the UK was worth nearly £76 billion. But, as we all know, visitor numbers can vary from one year to the next depending on national and world events. In 2002 the highest number of overseas visitors (15%) came from the USA but the conflict in Iraq and the SARS outbreak in Asia have since had a significant impact on visitors from both the USA and the East. We found this filtered down to us with the number of visitors we received from Europe having increased whereas those from the USA have been almost non-existent.

In the future it is anticipated that Britain may benefit from the impact of the USA visa requirement, leading to a potential increase in the home market and yet more visitors from Europe.

Although the bed and breakfast share of the market might appear small in percentage terms it is growing steadily. In some areas of the country there is a shortage of accommodation and shortly after we started operating there was a drive by our local Tourist Board to encourage participants.

---

[1] United Kingdom Tourism Survey (UKTS) and International Passenger Survey (IPS)

Accommodation used by UK residents and overseas visitors

	Overseas visitors %	UK residents %
Hotels/motels/guest houses	45	26
B&B	5	7
Free guest	39	47
Other	11	20

Most domestic visits are of short duration, from one to three nights. Our personal experience supports these statistics as we have found our British holidaymakers are invariably on short leisure or family breaks and our overseas guests are on touring holidays spending a few nights in each location. This suits us very well – the guest who spends two or three nights under our roof is our ideal choice.

Duration of all Tourism Trips 2002

	UK residents % of trips	Overseas residents % of visits
1 night	30	14
2 nights	27	14
3 nights	14	12
4 nights	9	10
5 nights	5	6

Although Easter to early autumn is the most popular time for breaks the seasonal nature of tourism is not as apparent statistically as might be expected. The retired have freedom of choice and many workers now favour taking short vacations throughout the year. Couples enjoy leisure breaks without children and with smaller families the number of years during which parents are restricted to school holidays is reducing. Unfortunately our experience does not bear these figures out, our occupancy rate from January to March being much lower than these statistics suggest. This may be because we are in a semi-rural location and city breaks, particularly in places such as London, York and Edinburgh, may distort the picture.

Seasonality of trips

	UK residents % of trips	Overseas visitors % of trips
Jan, Feb, Mar	21	19
Apr, May, Jun	26	26
Jul, Aug, Sep	29	31
Oct, Nov, Dec	24	24

There is undoubtedly scope for providing B&B accommodation right across the UK. However, the geographical distribution of tourists is highly variable, with overseas visitors strongly favouring London and the South East, whereas domestic travellers make greater use of the wilder, more scenic areas.

Geographical distribution

	Overseas tourism nights (millions)	Domestic tourism nights (millions)
Cumbria	1.0	13.0
Northumbria	3.9	13.4
North West	9.5	39.3
Yorkshire	7.5	36.3
Heart of England	21.1	64.8
East of England	13.6	44.3
London	75.4	35.4
South West	11.5	87.1
South East	31.4	77.3
Southern	unspecified	45.8
Scotland	15.0	64.5
Wales	6.6	39.8
Northern Ireland	1.7	9.3

POTENTIAL HOSTS

Social trends are bringing about a new and evolving pool of B&B hosts who are looking for a more satisfying way of life coupled with an income and find supplying serviced accommodation integrates well with other commitments.

◆ **Retirees**. Where one or both partners have recently retired. With folks living longer and with the prospect of many years in healthy retirement it can be helpful to have something to supplement the pensions. For most of us our home is our greatest asset and making an income from a property too large and/or expensive for two is an alternative to downsizing. Not only will it help with cash flow but there are additional bonuses in keeping a family home going with plenty of accommodation when the children and grandchildren return for holidays and festivities – particularly important with scattered and extended families.

Whereas one option is to utilise an existing property, another is to sell up in an expensive area and buy a larger property in a part of the country where houses are cheaper but which has an appeal for tourists. We have come across several retirees who have moved from the South East to Scotland or the West Country and set up a hobby B&B; their lifestyle change being for both personal and financial reasons.

◆ **Home workers**. A rapidly growing number of Britons now work from home. Self-employment increased by 9% in 2003 and others are now on contract work, which does not guarantee a regular income. Folks who fall into this category cover a wide range of employment: those in artistic occupations; such as writers, musicians, photographers, artists and craft workers; those in the construction industry such as carpenters, electricians, painters and decorators and those offering complementary health and beauty services such as massage therapists, reflexologists, counsellors and beauticians.

Similarly, an expanding workforce is spending much of their working day at home on computers, translating, researching or investing, able to do so because of the improvements in technology with the internet, e-mail and word processing. Those employed in these 'flexible' occupations are often in a position to host visitors on a relatively small scale and welcome this secondary income to balance the peaks and troughs of their main occupation.

♦ **Down shifters**. There is a steady flow of young entrepreneurs, many still in their thirties and forties, who are choosing to move away to the countryside in search of a more fulfilling and leisurely way of life both for themselves and their families. Redundancies in the financial sector have given them the cash to reevaluate their lifestyles. Many have paid off their mortgages and find themselves in a position to seek a more satisfying existence such as combining a smallholding or other rural occupation with a modest B&B business.

♦ **Full-time parents/carers**. If one partner, or a single parent, remains at home to care for children there may be an opportunity to combine this with B&B and the top-up income it promises. Perhaps of all the intending hosts these are the ones who need to think through the potential problems as the demands of the children will have to come second to those of the guests and the two are not necessarily compatible. It does not present a very professional image if your telephone or door is answered by a 6-year old, and whereas some visitors may love having your youngsters around for others it could become an issue.

FINANCIAL CONSTRAINTS

Whether there are financial risks will depend very much on where you are coming from. Generally B&B will be viewed as a low risk financial option but we all expect to operate our businesses at a profit.

The three main issues are:

♦ **Do you need to replace earned income?** With a maximum of three letting bedrooms this is not really an option if you have to live solely on the proceeds unless you can offer a very high-class product with additional services – such as a home hospitality package. The 'six guest' concession is really for the benefit of those entering the hospitality industry because they see it as something enjoyable which will also supply a top-up income and provide some savings on their own household expenses such as hot water, light and heat, the cost of which will be partly covered by the guests.

♦ **Will you be adapting an existing property?** Depending on what facilities are already in place you may wish to make structural changes, such as putting in en-suite bathrooms, clearing an area of the garden for additional parking, converting a dining room or including facilities for the disabled. There should be no need for any great capital outlay in the initial stages but depending on how successful the venture is you could introduce improvements at a later date. We chose to put in en-suite bathrooms before we started but knew it would increase the value of our property even if the venture failed.

♦ **Will you be buying a new property to serve the B&B market?** Those investing in a new property, bought specifically for this purpose, are unlikely to recoup their capital investment. If the property is already operating as a B&B some of the advertising may already be in place and you should also get feedback from the vendor regarding level of takings, which is helpful in budgeting.

If adapting your existing home, or buying new, you may need to take out a loan to cover the costs and in this event your bank manager will need a business plan.

CREATING A BUSINESS PLAN

However low-key the operation a simple business plan will provide a focus for analytical thinking even if you do not need to borrow money. Should you need a loan it will demonstrate that you have assessed the viability of your ideas with realistic figures of how much you will be spending and what you might expect in return. The figures you present can only be provisional but once you have been running for a year you will have a clearer idea of your occupancy rate and how you can adjust your costs.

Whether you need to make structural changes or not you will still need to estimate and list your start-up expenses (see Figure 1). To meet the necessary standards you may have to fit locks on bedroom and bathroom doors, replace your hot water tank for one with a larger capacity, replace carpets or curtains and add to your stock of pillows, bed linen, towels, crockery and cutlery. Indeed you may need a small business loan just to cover start-up costs.

SOCIAL CONSIDERATIONS

The essence of B&B is that accommodation is supplied in a family home with visitors looked after by the family – it is a home first and business second. The over-riding consideration is whether you, and the rest of your family, will be comfortable sharing your

Item	Details	£
Building alterations/ additions		
Decoration		
Furniture		
Linen/towels		
Accessories, e.g. hostess trays		
China/cutlery		
Bathroom supplies		
Tourist Board membership		
Brochures and stationery		
Advertising		
Setting up website		
Additional insurance		
Professional fees – accountant, solicitor		

Fig. 1. Estimated setting-up costs.

home in this way. If you are flustered by having to change your regime to accommodate that of others, irritated by minor mishaps such as mud on the carpet or ring marks on the furniture, or find it difficult to trust strangers, then B&B is probably not for you. You will find the presence of strangers disruptive so will not enjoy the experience and neither will your guests.

If this is to be a joint effort it is advisable to delineate responsibilities in advance. It is all too easy for one partner to become resentful if they feel they are shouldering the bulk of responsibility and having to sacrifice a game of golf simply because guests arrive late for breakfast. This can lead to heated exchanges in the kitchen or black looks in the dining room – neither of which is endearing to your visitors.

Hosts should be prepared for business curtailing their social lives. For instance, by taking advance bookings you might have to refuse an invitation to a wedding or the opportunity of a holiday because you are already committed to a Saturday night booking. Similarly, entertaining or going out can sometimes be problematic if you are waiting for guests to arrive. Whilst this can be frustrating you are free to work out your own strategy and it is this freedom that allows us to say 'no' when it is not convenient to take guests that we find so appealing.

The law makes a distinction between a 'hotel' and a 'private hotel' with B&Bs being classified as 'private hotels'. The big advantage of a 'private hotel' is that you can pick and choose your guests even if you have beds available (providing you are not discriminating on the basis of disability, gender or race), so you are at liberty to turn business away.

On the other hand, if you want as many bookings as possible somebody needs to be on call most of the day, and certainly in the late afternoon, in case a potential client phones. Someone will also need to be at home during the mornings as many guests like a late breakfast, particularly at weekends. Admittedly we have found most visitors, once over the threshold, will adapt quite happily to our prior commitments but we don't feel it is fair to impose our regime on them when they are on holiday unless it is unavoidable.

Potential irritants

You may be asked for early breakfasts, even at weekends. Guests have planes to catch and work commitments to meet so you need to be prepared to be well presented and sociable early in the morning. Five am is the earliest we have served breakfast, but my husband breathed a thankful sigh when the guests turned down the offer of a cooked meal. By contrast, other visitors will be night owls so if you cannot sleep until the front door is finally double locked for the night you may find hosting too stressful.

Another potential irritant is having to keep the house tidy – all the time. We get very few 'cold callers' but it is embarrassing to have people standing on the doorstep wanting to view the room and knowing the bedroom doors are open, the beds unmade and there are toys spread across the landing.

FEARS

Friends are often surprised at how cavalier we are towards handing out the keys to our home to folks we don't know. The fears they express include invasion of privacy, helping themselves to your property, abusing your 'nice' things, wetting the bed, and throwing up over the carpet. Although we have had limited experience we have found that guests behave in an exemplary manner and have never made unreasonable demands.

However, we do remember our very first visitors – a young couple with spiky hair and interesting piercings. We locked our bedroom door, craned our ears to hear if they were creeping round the house during the night and almost expected to find the house trounced next morning. As it happened they appeared for breakfast at the requested time, were charming and left their rooms in good order. It was a timely lesson in not being judgemental.

We try to generate a feeling of mutual trust and guests, feeling they are being accepted as friends, behave as any good friend would. Nearly all our guests leave the house after breakfast and do not return until early evening. Once in their rooms we have found they are concerned that the television in their bedroom may be bothering us! We have never had a problem with anything going missing and other operators with many more years experience than us have confirmed this.

As a private proprietor you have no right to confiscate a guest's property for non-payment of the bill (hoteliers have this right of lien). But this is negative thinking – unless you are particularly unfortunate the last thing your guests will have in mind will be to skip off without paying. The nearest we have come to a guest taking advantage was when a young lady booked a single room to attend a wedding at a local castle and then brought back a male companion in the early hours. On coming down to breakfast she realised she couldn't secrete him out without us seeing. She was suitably embarrassed, paid for a double and left without breakfast – we still have a drop-pearl earring as a souvenir.

We have never experienced any deliberate damage, though accidents will happen and you will have to tolerate the occasional scratches on the furniture and the walls on the stairwell getting marked with luggage. To compensate for a few wear and tear scuffs we have found there are many pluses. You will gain control of your life – no boss making unreasonable demands and no more commuting – work is now literally on your doorstep. You can operate when you want to and holiday when you choose.

LOCATION

The first pointer to the type of customer you are likely to attract is your location and the nature of the neighbourhood. If you are surrounded by National Trust properties, period homes and ornamental gardens you are likely to attract tourists. If you are in or near a university town or the catchment area of a public school, visiting academics and parents of students are a likely source. Those in the centre of cities will find visitors attracted by the theatres, art galleries, museums and shopping together with commercial customers with business to transact.

In the countryside riding or walking may be the draw, whilst the dales and mountains will attract hikers, climbers and cyclists. Those situated within walking distance of any of the long distance footpaths such as the Offa's Dyke Path, the Pilgrim's Way or Hadrian's Wall will find these a source of custom. We have hosted walkers trekking the Vanguard Way on a number of occasions. The coast and lakes will attract those who enjoy water sports, fishing and bird watching. Theme parks and zoos will attract families and all areas will appeal to motorists whether pursuing a hobby such as photography, local history or archaeology or just generally enjoying the sights.

Close proximity to a motorway, railway or airport can be in your favour if guests wish to travel but a disadvantage if they are looking for somewhere quiet to chill out. Those looking to buy a property will have greater freedom of choice and need to look at what will bring people to the area and for how many months of the year. Bear in mind that traditional British visitor destinations such as the Lake District, Wales, Scotland and the West Country will have a short tourist season compared with the towns and cities. Your location will also influence the continuity of business. Those relying on tourists will run a more seasonal operation, and repeat bookings are less likely.

Your nearest tourist information office will have the knowledge to fill you in on local demand – if there is little it is unlikely you will be able to start a viable business however desirable your property and however much advertising you do. Forgive the cliché but 'location, location, location!' is still the key to success. The good news is that there is scope in most towns and throughout rural Britain.

PREMISES

Bearing in mind the greater sophistication of the average traveller you will need to think about what is likely to bring customers over your threshold rather than that of your competitors. Look at the competition. Are there plenty of commercial places around? Are there similar establishments in the area? If not maybe you will be filling a gap in the market but check this out as it looks suspicious if no one else has seen the business opportunity.

On the other hand, if you find there are already a large number of similar establishments don't necessarily be put off as a glut in an area can boost business. When we are touring we would choose to visit a village where we knew there were half-a-dozen or so accommodation possibilities rather than a hamlet where there was only one. As with other businesses, antique shops come to mind, grouping can be an advantage and there may well be enough business for everyone – it will be up to you to establish a competitive edge.

Every guest has different priorities but plus points are a home of architectural or historic interest; an attractive setting or good view; pleasing external appearance of property and garden; potentially quiet location without too much traffic noise; off street parking for cars – particularly in urban areas; availability of an evening meal and use of leisure facilities such as a swimming pool or tennis court. We are fortunate in overlooking farmland and an American lady inspecting our double bedroom was immediately won over when she saw the flock of sheep just beyond the garden fence and exclaimed excitedly to her husband 'Look honey, woollies!'.

WHO WILL BE YOUR CUSTOMERS?

If you are providing a traditional B&B your potential clientele are likely to be looking for economically priced rooms and/or more personal service than they would receive in a hotel or travel lodge. Whatever the initial reasoning visitors are more likely to be well travelled than a few years ago and increasingly discerning.

Overseas tourists

With the present exchange rate on currency the more reasonable prices asked for B&B, together with the opportunity to see the inside of a British home and chat to the host family, are a great attraction to those from overseas. The expansion of regional airports and budget flights is likely to see visitors from overseas venturing beyond the usual popular areas of London, the Cotswolds and Edinburgh. We are fortunate to be within an hour's drive of Gatwick airport and the Channel Tunnel terminal so accommodate a number of foreign visitors often at the start or end of their vacations.

About 70% of our visitors during our first summer were from abroad, mainly Europe, but others were from Canada, South Africa, Australia and the USA. Regrettably, with the rate of exchange and concerns about terrorism, the number of long-distance travellers has fallen off during the last few years.

Domestic market

The domestic market embraces both holidaymakers and those visiting family and friends. It accounts for much of the weekend trade with guests attending 21st, wedding, silver, ruby and golden anniversary celebrations. There is also a sad side – local residents needing to accommodate family during terminal illness and funerals.

This locally generated business is supported by recent research which has revealed that visits to friends and relatives, who live too far away for a day trip, has increased by a third in the last five years and in 2002 nearly 40 million UK residents made overnight visits to friends and relatives generating £3,428m of spending. With the smaller size of modern houses many of these travellers need to stay in hotels, guest houses or B&Bs. We frequently host grandparents who find the cramped conditions and early mornings spent with their families too taxing, or sons and daughters visiting their parents in local residential homes.

House seekers, some at the viewing stage and others who need accommodation for a few days whilst they move, are another source of guests. There are some stately homes in our area and we have found stallholders showing at antique and craft fairs have supplied us with a regular clientele on particular weekends over several years.

As many B&Bs are cheaper than commercial establishments you should be aware you may be approached by separating couples, casual manual workers employed in the area or DSS clients. Such guests often bring 'baggage' and may not fit in with your vision. If this is something you would not be at ease with it is helpful if you have worked out a strategy in advance. We prefer not to have guests for more than a few days and if they request longer we make more detailed enquiries and if we feel it appropriate direct them to alternative accommodation. On a couple of occasions we have had to encourage single men who have booked in from Monday to Thursday to move on, suggesting that something more permanent, such as a bed-sit or flat share, would be appropriate. Others may particularly like these clients as they leave the weekends free for leisure guests.

Not all guests will fit in with your expectations. How would you feel if a couple of teenagers request a double bed or when two women or two men specifically request a double bed when there is a twin available? If this is something you would be uncomfortable with you need to be prepared with an answer. Similarly if you are hosting guests as a single person you may feel ill at ease with single travellers of the opposite sex. These are all issues that need to be thought about as it is against the law to discriminate.

We have hosted a wide spectrum from honeymoon couples to guests sponsored by the British Legion and find part of the excitement is never knowing who will be next over the threshold. It is this opportunity to embrace other cultures and discuss people's occupations, interests and circumstances that has provided us with an insight into worlds we previously knew little about.

Commercial market

Business customers accounted for 30% of UK income from tourism in 2003 and this is forecast to grow to 45% by 2010. Regrettably this is an area where there is still an image problem. Those employed in large companies tend to view their personal status, and that of the company they are working for, according to the perceived standard of accommodation in which they stay. In their pecking order B&B is budget accommodation and at the bottom of the list. Our experience of business clientele has been mainly with the self-employed or those engaged in new business ventures anxious not to waste the company's resources. There is scope for a PR and marketing exercise here to bring corporate clients into the twenty-first century!

For those who establish a business hosting corporate clients there will be repeat bookings from those looking for a more homely environment and we have found business women, travelling alone, often express their preference for the security of a family run bed and breakfast.

Home hospitality

There is an expanding niche market for hosts living in suitable
privately owned houses to offer a complete hospitality package –
bed and breakfast, picnic lunches, afternoon tea and evening meal,
all served to the guests as though they were personal friends of the
family.

The best-known British consortium of privately owned houses
offering this package is Wolsey Lodges. They have over 200
properties registered on their books in the UK together with
branches throughout Europe. The properties are often of
historical or architectural interest, such as converted mills,
granaries and schools, and might include anything from medieval
almshouses to Victorian manors. Each property tends to have
some unique feature to offer such as outstanding views, several
acres of well-kept gardens, a lake for fishing, a swimming pool or
a tennis court. In addition these private homes are usually
furnished to an exceptionally high standard often with antique
furniture, quality paintings and four-poster beds.

The level of service reflects the generous hospitality you might
expect to lay on for friends. So guests may be entertained to tea
and homemade cakes in the drawing room on arrival, followed by
pre-dinner drinks taken by a log fire, and the evening meal served
in the family dining room with the hosts joining the guests for
dinner. The hosts offering this service often have a particular
interest or skill in cooking, such as Cordon Bleu qualifications,
and specialise in imaginative homemade dishes using the best of
local produce. The prices for this sort of accommodation will of

course match the service provided. Bed and breakfast is likely to be £30–£65 per head (plus single supplement if applicable) and an evening meal from £15 to £35 per head. If you possess, or plan to buy, the right property and have the time and inclination to share your home so fully it is likely to lead to the greatest returns, but requires a high level of commitment and could make heavy inroads into your private life. A difficult customer who is with you overnight can be tolerated; one who is with you for 24 hours over several days might be a different matter.

Depending upon facilities, and the host's interests or expertise, there are openings for those offering home hospitality to provide additional attractions for which there is an extra charge. Examples are: fishing with hire of tackle; hire of bicycles; guided tours of the locality or with a bias towards special interests such as churches or gardens; golf or fishing instruction or classes in cooking, painting, needlework or any other marketable skill you possess.

Farm stay
This is another niche market for those living on working farms who have the facilities to host guests and provide additional facilities such as farm walks, watching the cows being milked and in some cases participating in the activities of a working farm. Many of these working farms are registered with Farm Stay UK Ltd.

Established B&Bs

Include in your research visits to other B&Bs in different areas
and serving different markets. Find out what they do well and
where you think you could make improvements. We have stayed in
B&Bs in Ireland, Scotland, Wales, France, Germany, South Africa
and New Zealand and always take the opportunity to use this
form of accommodation at least once a year.

LIKELY REASONS FOR FAILURE

◆ An unsuitable property that does not provide the necessary
  standard of accommodation;
◆ lack of market research into local demand;
◆ too high expectations of income;
◆ an unwillingness to really share your home.

Complying with the Law

VisitBritain publishes the *Pink Booklet – A Practical Guide to Legislation for Accommodation Providers*. This is an indispensable guide to the regulations relevant to those in the business of providing accommodation, covering the responsibilities of proprietors and where appropriates their rights. As this is a comprehensive publication embracing hotels, guest houses, self-catering, camp and caravan sites as well as B&Bs, not all the information is relevant. The following paragraphs are an overview; highlighting the legal formalities you need to think about before starting a business as well as your day-to-day responsibilities once you are operating. They should not be taken as a definitive guide to the law.

All hosts must comply with the legal requirements and those who enter their properties into the National Quality Assessment Scheme sign a code of conduct agreeing to meet all statutory obligations. Where there is flexibility, because of the 'six guest' concession, it is still prudent to follow the guidelines particularly where the safety of your guests is concerned.

THE 'SIX GUESTS' CONCESSION

Anyone who offers food and accommodation on a commercial basis has a responsibility to protect the public, and with this comes a plethora of legal obligations. But take heart for six guests (or three bedrooms) are the magic numbers – within this threshold you will have less formal responsibilities and some mandatory procedures will be simply advisory. For instance it is unlikely you will have to pay business rates, as you will be classified as a domestic rather than commercial property. Neither will you have to obtain a fire certificate with all the potential expense this involves with supplying equipment and possibly fitting fire doors and fire escapes; nor will it be compulsory to fit safety glass.

This more commonsense approach towards the small operator means reduced set-up costs and less form filling. That said there is still a range of legislation that is both relevant and evolving for those providing serviced accommodation.

PERMISSION TO OPERATE

If you are planning structural changes, as with any private property, you will have to apply for planning permission. 'Change of use' should not be necessary but local authorities vary in their requirements and those living in Northern Ireland will need a clearance letter from the planning authority. Even if you are planning to keep within the 'six guest' concession it would be advisable to contact your local authority on an informal basis. Considerations are the number of bedrooms, parking arrangements and possible effect on neighbours. Parking could be a particular issue for those in towns with restricted parking spaces. If the property you intend to use is rented or leasehold you will need to check there are no restrictive terms in the lease or rent agreement.

COMPLYING WITH REGULATIONS

Signing

Your local planning authority can give formal and informal advice on the placing of signs advertising your business or directional signs on the approach roads. Generally speaking, unless you live in a listed building or conservation area, it is permissible to put a non-illuminated sign within the grounds of your own property without the need to obtain planning consent – known as 'deemed consent'. Fully illuminated signs always require planning permission, partially illuminated ones may and local authorities can place restrictions on the size. If you live off the beaten track you may well wish to erect directional signs, and for these you will always need the express consent of the highways department of your local planning authority.

Council tax – business rating

If you remain within the 'six guests' concession and do not carry out major structural changes to your property you will not be required to pay business rates if this is your sole residence and B&B use is subsidiary to private use.

Fire certificate

With six or fewer guests (to include living in staff but not family) a fire certificate is unnecessary unless some of the accommodation is to be found above first floor level, below ground level or you live in Northern Ireland. But be aware, if you are tempted to squeeze in an extra guest or two on a temporary bed it will be an offence to use your premises without a fire certificate and any public liability insurance you have may be rendered invalid in the event of a fire. Similarly, those with more than six bed spaces who claim never to accommodate more than six people at any one time do not take in the fire authorities!

Although a fire certificate isn't compulsory hosts still have a responsibility for the safety of their guests. You should work out ways to supply some means of early warning, a way of calling the fire service and provision for a safe escape. It is prudent, therefore, to install smoke detectors, have a fire extinguisher available and have planned emergency evacuation procedures – particularly important when the property has security locks on doors and windows.

Private water supply

B&B providers with a private water supply must have it tested by the Environmental Health Department to ensure its safety. This department also holds literature relating to the law in this field.

Health and safety

Everyone wants to prevent accidents and all hosts have a 'duty of care', under the Occupiers' Liability Act, for the safety of their guests and the public, and can be held responsible if a visitor is injured due to the negligence of the proprietors or others acting on their behalf. This means you will have to be vigilant over loose wires, worn carpets and items left in areas where they could become a hazard.

Food standards

Irrespective of any legal requirements you will, of course, wish to maintain consistently high standards of food safety and hygiene to protect your guests from food poisoning. Under the Food Safety Act 1990 all B&B businesses, however small or casual, are required to register with their local authority. Registration is free and requires the completion of a simple form obtainable from the Environmental Health Department. Officers from the department have the right to inspect premises at any reasonable time without making an appointment. However, since sending in our form seven years ago there has been no contact, which I understand is because the nature of the food served in B&Bs is not deemed to be high risk. However, if there were a complaint I'm sure they would immediately be knocking at our door.

The Food Safety Regulations 1995 require all food operations to be carried out in a hygienic way with premises and equipment clean and well maintained. The raw ingredients should be of good quality with the safety of food guaranteed by ensuring it is maintained at the specified maximum or minimum temperatures. Personal and kitchen hygiene must be of a high standard. In practice this includes thorough washing of hands before food preparation, covering abrasions, no smoking, keeping pets out of the kitchen, covering all food, keeping separate chopping boards for raw meat and bread, washing all fruits which may be eaten raw and keeping the refrigerator below 5°C.

As local Environmental Health Officers are responsible for health and safety in B&Bs you can always contact them for advice. In particular they can refer you to food handling training courses being held locally, and if available 'Good Hygiene Awards' given to those deemed to be operating above the legal minimum standards.

EMPLOYMENT

Should you decide that changing the beds and cleaning two or three rooms is too much like hard work you may be tempted to employ a part-time cleaner or someone to help with the breakfast. Although only on a part-time basis this cannot now be treated as 'cash in hand' to be paid out as and when there is a need. You will find yourself in an area affected by employment legislation and will have to comply with a number of statutory obligations designed to protect the interests of employees.

For instance, under the Contracts of Employment Act if your 'girl Friday' works for more than eight hours a week she will be entitled to a written statement of the main terms and conditions of employment – to include pay, holidays, hours, sick pay, pension arrangements and grievance and disciplinary procedures. This is now backed up by a statutory requirement for three weeks paid holiday per annum. You will be obliged to pay at least the national minimum wage, currently £4.50 per hour for those over

22 and unless your cleaner is self-employed you may have to keep full records and make the necessary reductions for tax and NI if applicable.

Employers must also comply with the Health and Safety at Work Act by providing a safe environment in which to work – also useful for guests! Should you fail to have that kettle fixed (you know its funny ways and have lived with it for months) and your cleaner scalds herself she is entitled to claim, so back this up with employers' liability insurance against any claim for liability for injury or illness. Checking out your responsibilities towards employees is particularly important nowadays as more and more people are juggling several part-time jobs to achieve a full-time wage. Advice can be obtained from the local Job Centre, Citizens' Advice Bureau or on the internet.

INSURANCE

The first priority is to prevent personal injury, theft or damage and the second is to be adequately insured. Even with a maximum of six guests it is unlikely that your household cover will be sufficient, as the policy will assume your home is occupied by family only and is likely to include restrictions on what can be claimed. If a spark from the fire burns a hole in your sitting room carpet the fact that you now take paying guests may invalidate your claim because you have withheld a 'material fact' even though your visitors were not involved in the accident. Similarly, if a guest helps themselves to the radio in their bedroom any claim may fail because your household policy restricts claims to forced entry only.

Public liability cover is not compulsory but has to be a high priority bearing in mind the current trend for claiming for any personal injury, however sustained, and is essential if you participate in the National Quality Assurance Standards scheme.

With these potential risks it is advisable to inform your insurance company of the change in circumstances before you start operating, as you may need to add extra cover to an existing policy or take out a package designed for accommodation providers. There are brokers who specialise in this field and offer carefully thought out policies and support. Don't be too concerned over cost. We kept our existing building's insurance but took out a specialist package for contents and to cover all legal requirements and found the premium was only 10% higher than our previous household policy.

Areas in which you need to be confident you have cover in the event of a claim are:

◆ Personal injury claims – will you be covered if a paying guest or employee slips on a highly polished floor and breaks their leg?

◆ Accidental damage to house and contents.

◆ Theft by a guest – will you be covered if a guest steals your silver candlesticks or the property of other guests staying in the B&B? (Generally speaking as a 'private' hotel you will only be responsible for a guest's luggage if there was some negligence on your part – hence the need for locks on guests' doors.)

TELEVISION LICENCES

The Television Licensing Authority requires everyone supplying TVs for the use of guests (including small B&Bs) to apply for a special 'hotel licence' known as the Hotel and Mobile Units Television Licence. The number of guest bedrooms in which TVs are installed determines the fee. This is not a problem as with less than 15 letting bedrooms the fee is the same as for a standard domestic licence and the same licence will cover your family TV sets.

BOOKINGS

A verbal contract exists once a host agrees to provide specific accommodation, on a certain date and at a specified price, and the guest agrees to take up and pay for same. This is legally binding but if it can be backed up in writing it makes any dispute much easier to deal with. In the event of a 'no show', or cancellation without reasonable notice, your statutory rights allow you to claim for loss of business. A claim will exclude certain expenses that have not had to be met, such as cost of food and heating. Generally speaking it is considered reasonable to claim two-thirds of the full price. Claiming is one thing, achieving a result can be more challenging. If letters by recorded delivery do not bring the desired result you will be entitled to claim through the small claims court, if you think it worth the hassle. Even if you have the satisfaction of a judgement in your favour this doesn't necessarily produce the money – although I suppose a moral victory is worth something. We have only once followed up a 'no show', and this was with a company booking. They paid up once we threatened to sue. One way to minimise the problem is to provide guests with a source of cancellation insurance.

Proprietors are equally committed, and must also honour any prior booking agreed verbally with a guest, unless there are legal grounds for not doing so. If they fail they will be in breach of contract and the guest can claim damages for expenses incurred in finding alternative comparative accommodation – though probably not the deluxe hotel with the championship golf course! In our experience if a double booking has accidentally occurred the offending hosts will take responsibility for finding alternative accommodation.

VISITORS' REGISTER

One essential for everyone supplying accommodation in return for payment is the provision of a visitors' register. Under the Immigration (Hotel Record) Order 1972 it is necessary to keep a record of the name (address not essential but a useful tool) and nationality of all guests over 16 years of age. Additionally, all non-British, Irish and Commonwealth guests need to supply their passport number (or other document which shows their identity and nationality) and place of issue. Before departure they should also supply details of their next destination including the address if known. These records must be kept for 12 months and made available for inspection by the police if required.

We bought a three columned address/telephone book and changed the title of the last column to 'passport number' but in practice many guests have ignored this and used the last column for comments so it wasn't fulfilling its purpose. On the advice of our Quality Assessment inspector we have now created our own loose-leaf register, some of which we complete from the original booking taken over the phone (see Figure 2). We have kept the visitor book going as well as this is in the guest's own handwriting – and it's gratifying to have their comments.

It may seem like a simple request to ask a visitor from overseas to fill in their name, passport number and likely next destination – but not necessarily so. We handed our registration form to a couple from Europe when they booked in for a few days. When it wasn't returned we had to ask for it back whereupon our guest retorted that in 20 years staying in B&Bs in the UK he had never been asked to supply this information before, and would never give his address to anyone in the UK. (His rational was that he had heard that if you give your address in Britain you were liable to be burgled whilst away from home.) We gently pointed out the legal requirement, that there was no obligation to supply his home address and if he gave his next destination as Windsor Castle we really weren't in a position to challenge it. This was all carried out with good humour on our part but he could not be persuaded and we failed to get the necessary documentation. We recorded the circumstances should there be any comeback and have discussed it with the Quality Assessment inspector but have not as yet established how much teeth the law has in this instance.

Registration Form

Name ....

Address ....

....

Post code ....

Telephone no ....

Car registration no ....

Nationality ....

For all-non British guests
Passport no ....

Place of issue ....

Next destination (with address if known) ....

....

....

Arrival date ....

Departure date ....

On the back of the form we print:

Reasons for stay ....

Where they heard about us ....

Additional notes ....

E.g. 'Need extra blankets'; 'Have family living in area'.

Fig. 2. Sample registration form.

DATA PROTECTION

The information you collect from your guests for registration purposes is protected by the Data Protection Act. You will need to notify the Data Protection Commissioner if this is retained on a computer and you intend to use it for anything other than personal advertising.

TRADE DESCRIPTIONS ACT

The local Trading Standards Office can prosecute, and you could lay yourself open to a civil claim for misrepresentation, if you knowingly make false statements in any of your advertising or promotion. Hence care needs to be taken not to exaggerate the virtues of your property or its location.

NORTHERN IRELAND

Northern Ireland is ahead of the field in providing visitors with guaranteed minimum standards. It is a statutory requirement for all properties hosting B&B guests to be inspected. Prior to applying for inspection clearance letters are needed from the Fire Authority of Northern Ireland, Planning Service and the Environmental Health Department of the local District Council. Additionally the scale of charges for accommodation and services, together with the NITB Certificate, has to be displayed prominently in the entrance hall of the property.

Setting Up the Rooms: Décor and Equipment

First review what facilities you have and what you might need to acquire. With a six guest/three bedroom limit there are various permutations for bedrooms; a four bed family room, doubles, twins and singles.

Keep in mind this is first and foremost your home so decor and equipment will depend on your own individual style and taste. However, if redecorating or re-equipping the bedrooms you might choose to make some concessions to the main type of business you anticipate. For instance, business clients are likely to prefer simple modern furnishings with facilities for working in their rooms; overseas tourists are more likely to appreciate antique furniture and ornaments to fit with their vision of 'olde worlde'.

If you plan to use the marketing facilities of your Tourist Board and TICs, in our opinion essential, you will need to be guided by their quality standards towards the minimum specifications for facilities, furniture and equipment. Once their essentials have been satisfied, any additional facilities or improvements you can add will lead to a higher rating on the assessment scale.

BATHROOM FACILITIES

Private facilities, which should be adjacent or at least on the same floor, or en-suite, are increasingly sought after and this needs bearing in mind when deciding which rooms you plan to let. We have a twin and double, both en-suite, which are adjacent, so can also be let to families. We have a third double which we could let but as it is without its own bathroom we decided it would encroach too much on our privacy.

If visitors are to share bathroom facilities the establishment will only qualify for a rating if they meet the minimum requirements – at least one bath or shower and a separate WC for every six residents. If there are no washbasins in the bedrooms the WC must include a washbasin. When the maximum number in the household, including the family, is no more than six it is acceptable for guests to share the family bathroom but the personal belongings of the family should not be left in the bathroom and this joint use is becoming increasingly rare.

Either en-suite or private facilities are essential for five-diamond/star rating and very desirable if you wish to appeal to the overseas or upper end of the market. On a recent tour of Scotland we were interested to see how many established businesses had ploughed back their profits into building on rooms with en-suite toilets and showers. We also noted how variable these could be – anything from a large cupboard in the corner of the room with shower, washbasin and loo but no room for your knees or even to hang the towel, to spacious bathrooms with bath and individual shower. Our bedrooms are not large so we could not sacrifice losing any of this space. Fortunately the layout of our house enabled us to convert a third bedroom into two fair sized bathrooms.

DISABLED FACILITIES

The tightening of the disability discrimination laws in October 2004 require B&B providers to make 'reasonable adjustments' to their premises and the way they provide their services, to make them as accessible as possible to guests with disabilities. If you have an easily accessible ground floor room it would be worthwhile equipping it for disabled use by widening doorways, putting in ramps and supplying aids in the bathroom. This would certainly be seen as a plus factor when letting and a National Accessible Scheme has been set up by VisitBritain to meet the practical needs of wheelchair users and those with hearing and visual impairment. An additional consideration with ground floor letting bedrooms is security and privacy, so you may need to add extra bolts and blinds or net curtains.

BUILDING AND GARDENS

First impressions are so important. When touring we select initially from the guide book but the final choice depends on the outside of the house and its setting. For those who do not choose to make advance reservations but rely on B&B boards the choice will be strongly influenced by the welcoming exterior of the property and several times we have joined others in kerb crawling down a road in the late afternoon surveying the properties before making our final choice. A well maintained property with a colourful, cared for garden and drive in good repair is a definite draw. An easily identifiable front door, functioning bell and tidy porch are also desirable – it is very easy to overlook this area which can quickly be strewn with leaves if, like us, you use the back door for family use.

We would also emphasise the need for house numbers or names to be easy to spot from the road and read at night.

Although not an essential, guests appreciate somewhere to sit outside when the weather is warm. We have a bench seat in our sheltered front garden and a patio away from the house in the back garden where they can sit and relax with a drink without intruding on our privacy.

PARKING

To have adequate parking for all your guests is helpful. Two aspects to be borne in mind are security and carrying of luggage. We are fortunate in having ample parking near the house so there is no need for guests or family to shuffle their cars and we have a gate to our drive that we can close overnight. Understandably parking in built up areas can be difficult and you need to ensure your guests will not upset neighbours when parking their vehicles. If there is no parking on site, which may well be the case in towns and cities, guests will need information on local parking arrangements.

PUBLIC AREAS

Visitors will be received into the entrance hall and will use the stairs or corridors leading to the bedrooms and dining room. Safety in these areas is paramount so good lighting is essential above the front door and on the stairs and landings. Easily identifiable switches, preferably illuminated, will be helpful for guests returning to unfamiliar surroundings in the dark.

For immediate impact the entrance hall needs to be as tidy and uncluttered as possible. Although this is your home first it will pay dividends if the family collection of coats, umbrellas and outdoor shoes can be accommodated near the back entrance. The hall is also the place for fresh flowers, not only for visual effect but also the welcoming perfume.

The condition of carpeting on stairs and along corridors is often a cause for criticism from the Quality Assurance inspectors so this is an area not to be overlooked when refurbishing.

Telephone

Very rarely will a guest ask to use the telephone; we assume this is because the majority have their own mobiles. On the rare occasions they do we don't charge but invariably find a £1 coin left by the phone – well in excess of the actual cost. Just recently we have had one or two enquiring about checking their e-mails – no problem except our computer is in a part of the house which is usually off limits and not always very tidy.

BEDROOMS

The bedroom is the most important room for your guests and they will appreciate a warm, quiet, well-ventilated room without too much light in the early mornings, in which they feel safe. The Quality Assurance minimum standards require sufficient space to allow freedom of movement for guests, with a ceiling height that allows a person of 6ft (183cms) to move around the major part of the room without stooping – so check out those bedroom eaves. Their recommended minimum space for a single room is 60 sq ft (5.6 sq m), 110 sq ft (10.2 sq m) for a twin and 90 sq ft (8.4 sq m) for a double – in practice this means having access to a double bed from both sides.

Noise

We all get used to familiar noises and don't see them as a problem, but when sleeping in a strange bed sounds, or silences, take on unprecedented importance. One of our early visitors requested a clock – so we bought wall clocks for each room. But one guest removed their clock from the wall and put it out on the landing and on other occasions we have found the offending clocks in the wardrobe with a cushion on top! If a really quiet wall clock can be so upsetting imagine the frustration of a chiming grandfather clock in the hall. Eliminate as many noises as possible by insulating the room, remembering that heavy curtains, wallpapers and carpets help to absorb noise.

If starting from scratch well fitting doors and soundproofing of interior walls can go a long way to deadening sound. If external noise is the problem double or even triple glazing is worth considering.

Light and power

Plenty of natural light is always appreciated, except the early morning sun beaming in at 6am. The guidance given on artificial lighting is for a minimum of 160 watts for a single room and 220 watts for a double room with a light controllable from the door and another from the bed. This minimum is achieved with a high wattage central light and one (single) or two bedside lights. Power points will be needed for supplementary heating, hair dryers, mobile phones, laptops and television.

Heating

Effective levels of heating, with thermostatically controlled radiators, should be provided in each bedroom with extra heating available on request. Ambient heating is very personal and dependent on what guests are used to at home. We have had visitors staying during the winter months asking for the heating to be turned up, or left on all night, and yet come down to breakfast in T-shirts when we have been wearing jumpers. Aim to have the heating coming on about an hour before you expect your guests to arrive for breakfast at somewhere between 18-20 degrees for a universally acceptable temperature. Air conditioning or portable fans are appreciated in the summer.

Locks

These are needed on all bedroom doors so they can be secured from inside and out.

Flooring

Carpets help to absorb sound and if used should be of good quality and certainly in good condition. We opted for plain, light coloured carpets that might not seem the obvious choice. We have found that they look clean and this encourages guests to maintain them this way so they take off their shoes when they come in to the house, and wipe up spills immediately. I suspect if we had dark or patterned carpets they would not be so fastidious. If you opt for wood floors scatter rugs will be welcome by the side of the bed.

Furniture

When planning the furniture think about the length of time your guests are likely to stay and what they will need for maximum comfort. It does not seem sensible to use up precious floor space with wardrobes and chests of drawers that will probably never be used by those who only stay a few nights. The size and amount of furniture should be in proportion to the space available and to make the maximum use of our floor space every item of furniture had to work.

It helps to think about what a visitor might need to do in the bedroom. A business traveller may require a desk or table with appropriately sited plug where he/she can use their laptop; tourists may need to spread out maps and write holiday postcards; everybody will have some luggage that needs storing without obstructing access to the door or bathroom. Families may want to eat whilst they drink the beverages supplied on your hostess tray. Whatever you decide to include there are a number of essentials.

Beds

Comfortable good quality beds with bed heads. Don't be tempted to move your old bed into the guest room and have a new bed yourself. Today's travellers are very discerning and require high standards. Minimum sizes for Quality Assurance standards are 6ft 3ins × 4ft 6ins (190 × 137cms) for a double, and 6ft 3ins × 3 ft (190 × 90cms) for a single. If there is room to accommodate a queen-sized bed (plus bedside tables) in place of a double this is a bonus and a four-poster will add a touch of luxury. If buying new consider a hotel quality bed as these have reinforced edges that resist sagging, particularly useful if the bed is liable to be sat on to watch TV. Similarly, if buying new and you have the space many guests will appreciate a longer than standard length, but remember this will also mean longer than standard bed linen and covers – another expense.

Bunk beds, cots and high chairs
If you supply bunk beds, cots and high chairs they must be of British Standard quality. Children's beds in family rooms do not have to comply with the minimum size but bunk beds are only considered suitable for children.

Wardrobe and drawers
A wardrobe, freestanding or fitted, together with some drawers or shelves for folded items is essential. Quality Assurance will accept alcoves but not racks with hangers or hooks on the wall. We have found our guests do not require vast hanging space; indeed many never unpack at all. We have a small wardrobe in each room plus additional shelf and drawer space. You will need half a dozen or so matching hangers per guest. Wire hangers are not considered acceptable and you have to be vigilant and throw them out as

guests often leave them behind. A couple of hooks for outdoor clothes can be useful, particularly in wet weather. Drawers should have washable linings or be lined with appropriate paper.

Dressing table
Some form of table with a mirror adjacent is necessary. This need not be a dedicated dressing table and will often be more useful if it doubles as a writing table, which means a flat surface, kneehole space and suitably sited lighting.

Bedside table
Every guest must have access to a bedside table and light. In a double room there has to be two, though one between the beds is acceptable in a twin room.

Chairs
A comfortable chair is desirable for each guest. We solved this, in our limited space, by supplying tub chairs that slip under a round dining height table. These are often found in hotels but were not easily tracked down on the domestic market. Eventually we came up with some suppliers through the catering trade press.

Luggage rack
A luggage rack deters guests from putting their travel soiled luggage on the clean bed cover and where guests have to share bathrooms some form of rack for drying towels will be needed in the bedroom.

Soft furnishings

Curtains

You need to exclude light and provide privacy. Curtains should be lined with a professional looking finish and if an interlining can be included this will add to the quality as well as conserving heat.

Bedding

In our opinion it is essential to have a good quality, snug fitting, washable mattress protector to save your mattress, for just one accident can make a brand new bed suspect to any guest who chooses to pull back the sheets. Should we ever be asked we would justify the use by explaining it prevents house dust mites from breeding, a major cause of allergies. For comfort we add a thick, quilted polyester/cotton mattress cover.

Pillows

Some people have told us they are allergic to feather pillows whilst others don't like the squidgy polyester type – and the really fussy bring their own. We provide each guest with one feather pillow, with dust protector case, and one non-allergenic pillow, all with washable under slips. We have additional non-allergenic pillows available if asked.

Duvets or blankets

Some hosts provide a choice of blankets or duvets in their bedrooms. We currently supply duvets in our double room and blankets in the twin – so there is some element of choice. If supplying blankets Quality Assurance specify a minimum of two per bed. Extra blankets and different tog duvets kept in the rooms mean guests can help themselves should they need additional warmth.

Sheets and pillowcases

We use minimum iron all cotton but a mixture of cotton/polyester is acceptable provided they haven't started to wear thin. We have followed our hotel experience and stuck to white bed linen that has the advantage of being suitable for washing at high temperatures and can be bleached or boiled if necessary. It is also interchangeable between rooms so the initial outlay need not be so expensive. A minimum of three sets of bed linen per bed is recommended.

Additional requirements

Hospitality tray

This should hold a kettle, tea pot (optional), cups and saucers, tea bags, coffee, sugar and glasses for water/wine. It is seen as a plus if you provide bottled water and biscuits. We also supply a tea towel for guests' use between evening and morning cuppas. We provide fresh milk and it was suggested by our Quality Assessment inspector that this should be in an insulated jug – we comply with this request in warm weather. You will need to be particularly vigilant if offering biscuits or jiggers of milk that they are not out of date.

Waste paper basket

A waste paper basket with poly-bag lining for hygiene and

convenience in emptying should be kept next to the hostess tray to catch any drips from the used tea bag.

TV

A colour TV is more or less essential if there is no separate lounge; this need not be large but should have a zapper usable from the bed. It also needs to be sited so it is visible from both the easy chairs and bed. TVs hung from the wall tend to be frowned on as not providing the ambience of a home.

Other items

A full-length mirror and a hair dryer complete the list of essentials. A radio or clock/radio so guests can set their own alarms is a useful addition. We are happy to give visitors an early morning call if asked and suggest it for those who we suspect might sleep in!

Tourist information

A tourist information file should be placed in each bedroom. At a recent inspection it was suggested that this should start with a welcoming letter outlining essential information about the room, routine of the house, emergency procedures and what is available on the breakfast menu. This has proved helpful as we sometimes forget to verbally pass on essential information such as breakfast times and quirks in the hot water system.

As we don't have a guests' sitting room we have wall hanging bookshelves in the bedrooms on which we display guide books, local topographical books, books of walks and the history of the area together with general light reading.

Pictures (we include some of the local area), ornaments, cushions, rugs and personal effects add a homely touch, but can be overdone. During a recent B&B break in the north of England I decided I couldn't take any more graduation photos in prominent positions! We have put a book of favourite poems in both rooms, our secular alternative to the Bible, which has been favourably commented on on several occasions, one guest even using a poem she found for her sister's memorial service. We also try to leave a couple of up-to-date magazines in each room.

Finally, as everything in the bedroom should be solely for the comfort of your guests you will have to resist the temptation, even if the room is large and has ample cupboard space, to store items not specifically for their use.

See/hear/smell/touch/taste

The overall aim is that your guests should have a relaxing and enjoyable stay, so once your rooms are set up sleep in them for a couple of nights and use your five senses to judge what your guests will be experiencing.

- Does everything you see please you or could you alter the arrangement of the furniture?

◆ Is anything missing such as a place to plug in a hairdryer in front of a mirror or somewhere to dry your undies over night?

◆ Are there any unpleasant or disturbing noises you could eliminate from the plumbing or other users of the property whether family or other guests?

◆ Would double-glazing help to eliminate external noises?

◆ How intrusive is your TV?

◆ Would carpets or heavier curtains in the room below reduce the noise?

◆ Does everything smell fresh?

◆ Are the bed linen and towels soft to the touch?

◆ Pay particular attention to the heating, both the temperature of the room and the weight of the bedding – it's all too easy leaving folks sweltering under a 14 tog duvet when the temperature in the 70s.

◆ Finally are the items on your early morning tea tray fresh and water from the tap safe to drink and pleasant to taste?

BATHROOMS

Equipment

Bathrooms should contain a lidded WC, washbasin (minimum recommended internal size 14ins × 9.5ins), and some means for bathing. There are a number of acceptable alternatives for bathing: a bath (spa bath at the luxury end of the market) and separate shower unit, a bath with shower over or a shower cabinet. What is important is that the shower should be efficient – which means installing a power shower; and easy to operate – how many of us have stood under showers in foreign countries, sometimes freezing sometimes scalded, whilst we tried to understand the system? Shower screens on the side of the bath are preferable to curtains but if using shower curtains they need to be well weighted.

Privacy

Privacy can be assured with opaque glass or blinds at the windows. As the view from our bathroom windows is across farmland to the hills beyond we have plain glass and half net curtains but guests still pull the blinds down firmly though there is no one to see them but the sheep. A bolt should be fitted on the door.

Heating and ventilation

Some sort of heating is necessary for warmth and to dry the towels, either a radiator with rail above or heated towel rail. Even if you have windows that open extractor fans are invaluable in clearing the steam and preventing mould. If your en-suite is an internal room they will be essential.

Hot water

Make sure the tank is of sufficient capacity to supply all the hot water likely to be needed at peak times. With three rooms this could be half a dozen baths or showers between 7 and 8am. We had to double the size of our existing hot water tank and even then it's 'family hold back' and no using of the washing machine or dishwasher until after breakfast. Similarly for those not on main drainage check that the waste disposal system will be adequate to deal with the extra usage.

Flooring

Bathrooms are particularly prone to accidents so every step should be taken to protect your guests. Floor tiles should be non-slip; showers should have non-slip bases and handholds be provided on the bath. When used by the family our bathrooms were carpeted, but for reasons of hygiene we replaced these with washable floors, one tiled and one laminate. The laminate was a better choice being warmer and quieter.

Bathroom accessories

There should be a well-lit mirror above the basin and ideally a shaver point adjacent though it is acceptable for this to be in the bedroom. Additional items include a toilet roll holder, hooks for bath robes, shelves for storing guests' needs and Quality Assurance asks for a lidded waste bin. We also provide rubber non-slip mats for placing in the bath, a sponge and antiseptic cleaning materials should guests wish to make use of them, unbreakable tooth mugs and a spare toilet roll. We have found it helpful to have bathmats and shower curtains that are interchangeable between our two rooms rather than sticking to individual colour schemes.

Initially we supplied liquid soap and have been assured that this is quite acceptable and a cheaper option than individual wrapped soaps. However, having tracked down a supply of individually packaged soaps, shampoo and shower gel at out local cash and carry we offer these alongside quality branded makes in large bottles. (We haven't registered for a 'cash and carry' card but take along proof of trading, such as our current advert in the tourist guide, each time we wish to buy.) Other optional items are facial tissues, cotton wool balls and whatever else takes your fancy.

Towels
We supply white towels, two per person, for the same reasons that we provide white bed linen and on the recommendation of the inspector we now supply flannels, which about half of our clients use. This was good advice for us as well as they protect the towels from make-up.

DINING ROOM
Some hosts provide separate tables for each letting bedroom but this is not essential. Our guests use our family dining table so sometimes have to share with strangers. On the rare occasions when both rooms have chosen to eat at the same time they usually seem to get on well and sometimes enjoy the experience so much we cannot get them to move on. On one occasion the cultural

differences, which add spice to the experience, became apparent when a French and English couple were sharing and our French visitors poured their coffee into their cereal bowl, drank from the bowl and used it to dunk their croissants.

There seems little point in being too atmospheric at breakfast time, even the honeymoon couple are unlikely to be looking for soft lights and mood colours. A white starched cloth has an appeal, if somewhat formal, as does any pretty cotton cloth. Material napkins suggest luxury providing they are crisp and obviously laundry fresh. I am always suspicious of floppy checked seersucker that could have wiped the lips of half a dozen guests without it showing. If I think this way so might our visitors so we settle for good quality paper napkins as an alternative.

Co-ordinating china, for which you can get replacements, and good quality cutlery are a must. Both will need to withstand dishwasher temperatures With potentially four guests we need at least two coffee pots, two tea pots and two hot water jugs. We serve juice in small glass jugs holding about 2½ portions.

Soft background music can deflect the quietness and grumbles from the kitchen, and to have a morning paper available occupies guests travelling alone.

GUEST LOUNGE/SITTING ROOM

Some hosts are able to provide guests with their own sitting room where they can socialise with other visitors. This is a non-essential amenity that the majority of standard B&Bs in England do not offer, however it is expected in Northern Ireland although the room may be shared with the host family. For those who provide this facility the same criteria regarding quality of décor and furnishing apply as in the other public areas. Some establishments choose to have the television in the sitting room, others in bedrooms, or both. A supply of books and magazines are appreciated and if you welcome children this is the place for toys and board games.

We don't have the room to provide a separate lounge but each bedroom has space for a table and armchairs that can be used for watching television or writing. It also means we can serve continental breakfast in the room if requested. In the seven years we have been operating we have rarely been asked if we have a guests' sitting room so this hasn't proved to be a problem.

KITCHEN

Ideally this should be adjacent to the dining room and although not necessarily accessible to the guests we find ours often is. Visitors frequently have occasion to come into the kitchen to speak to us or take something from the fridge and as such it is almost a public area. In a hobby B&B the kitchen does not have to comply with commercial regulations but it is sensible to follow the guidelines voluntarily. We actually like to keep the kitchen door open to show we have nothing to hide! It is, of course, the area in which the Environmental Health department would be most interested and the Irish Tourist Board includes the kitchen in their schedule for assessment.

Appliances

With the extra laundry you may find it helpful to purchase a larger washing machine, tumble drier or commercial iron, but these can come later when you have some capital to plough back.

Looking After Your Guests

The minimum requirements are a safe environment, warm welcome, clean, comfortable accommodation and good food well cooked. The aim should be to meet, and if possible exceed your visitors' expectations.

SAFE ENVIRONMENT

In addition to complying with the legal obligations there are various precautions that can be taken to ensure your guests' personal safety and that of their possessions. Some categories of visitor are particularly at risk: the disabled, children who are sleeping separately from their parents and foreign tourists who may not speak the language.

To protect both people and property mortise locks to exterior doors, window locks and burglar alarms can be fitted. However, an easy exit from each bedroom, preferably through the main door but alternatively through a window, is essential, so bear this in mind if you have locked double glazed windows, or double locked doors and make sure guests have access to the keys.

Smoke alarms and fire extinguishers are recommended along with safety lighting outside the property and on stairways to help avoid accidents. Adaptors should be replaced with power boards and protruding objects at eye level, such as corners of cupboards, shelves and hooks avoided. Bathrooms are particularly fraught with hazards because of hard and slippery surfaces. The water should not be scalding hot and helpful safety aids should be added.

Even in what is to all intents and purposes a domestic property, guests should be informed of emergency evacuation procedures. Our Quality Assessment inspector suggested we include this in our 'welcome' letter, which accompanies the tourist information folder in each room. In our case these procedures meant placing a bell on the windowsill outside the guests' bedrooms to summon us in the event of an emergency during the night (they could also knock on our bedroom door!) and the whereabouts of the telephone with emergency numbers to ring. The Welsh Tourist Board requests that this should be available in a range of languages, or explained diagrammatically – something others might also like to consider particularly if they think it could be an issue because of the lay-out of their property.

Particular care needs to be taken over additional facilities, such as freedom to walk in the gardens where there may be a pond, children's play equipment or use of a swimming pool as these can raise additional safety issues. In case of accidents you should have available a first aid box, checked regularly to ensure it is complete. Apart from first aid it is probably unwise to get too involved with supplying advice or medication to guests.

FIRST CONTACT

Nearly all our bookings come by phone (sometimes indirectly through the local tourist office). At the time of booking we take the name, a contact telephone number and ask for anticipated time of arrival. We enter this information on the arrival date in the diary, add whether the customer wanted a twin or double and the date we took the booking which we then deem as confirmed. If customers want details of how to find us we explain over the phone if they are familiar with the area or take an address so that we can send a map. The approximate arrival time is important otherwise you will be waiting around unnecessarily or the guests will be left sitting outside your property not sure whether they are expected. It is also useful if a guest can notify you of any delay.

Should your house be difficult to locate the time honoured party idea of hanging balloons near the entrance, particularly for guests arriving in the dark, is worth considering.

We view the telephone conversation as an opportunity to build up a rapport with our guests and good communications at the time of booking help prevent misunderstandings over smoking, pets (yours and theirs), accessibility to services, etc. This is the time we ask about dietary requirements and without sounding too nosy try to find out why they are visiting the area as this might indicate whether we are their best choice. We live a mile from both the station and the town so are not ideal for guests without their own transport or for those who like to be within walking distance of eating places in the evenings. We like to be able to point this out in advance and if they still choose to come at least they know the situation.

As mentioned earlier another issue is how comfortable you will be with guests who want to stay long term, perhaps whilst working in the area or house hunting. This has never appealed to us and if we know in advance we refer them elsewhere. If we find that a potential guest seems to have an excessive number of requirements or expectations – in other words is fussy – we refer them to a hotel.

With only four bed spaces we can record bookings in a column in an A4 diary alongside our personal commitments so can see at a glance whether or not we are in a position to take a booking – well that's the theory! We also keep by the phone a list of alternative accommodation in the area if we are unable to supply what is requested. Sometimes this is because we are already booked and on other occasions because they want a particular type of room, which we cannot supply, such as a family or ground floor room.

We are very relaxed about taking bookings, which is not necessarily good practice as it can lead to misunderstandings. However, it does leave us with the minimum of paper work, which we prefer. We do not take deposits or ask for written confirmation, unless requested by the guest, relying on the fact that a verbal contract is a legal commitment. The future is likely to see many more bookings through the internet so confirmation will be much easier.

Supplying directions
A friend drew us two maps on his computer, one large scale showing our property in relation to the immediate area, and a second smaller scale map showing our town in relation to the

towns, motorways and airports and tourist sites within a 25-mile radius (see Figure 3). We include these with all written enquiries and have distributed them to the local tourist offices. It should be noted that maps need to be hand drawn or there could be copyright issues.

CANCELLATION POLICY

If you decide to adopt a cancellation policy, such as conditional or non-refundable deposits, this must be explained to guests when they first make contact and is a requirement of the Quality Assurance Code of Conduct. We have had a few cancellations over the years, some of which may not have happened if we had taken a deposit, but there has only been one instance of a guest failing to turn up. Although we feel able to adopt this casual approach to deposits the situation will be quite different with home hospitality packages where guests are expected for evening meals, the hosting is full-on and the chances of reletting the accommodation is low. In these cases a realistic deposit, carefully thought out cancellation policy and the offer of holiday cancellation insurance is probably essential.

Some guests, particularly those from Europe, like to see the bedroom before committing themselves and we always assume this with guests who come at short notice via our TIC. We haven't been turned down yet but prefer they should have a 'let out' if they are not happy with the accommodation on offer.

WELCOME

With apologies for stating the obvious – but the Quality

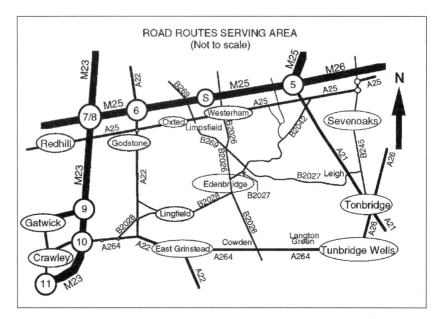

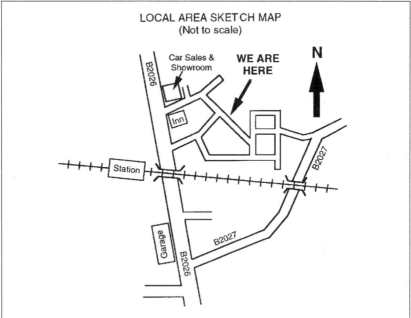

Fig. 3. Sample maps.

Assurance brochure makes a point of the need to be tidy, polite and helpful. Some hosts offer their guests a pot of tea or coffee with homemade cakes or scones on arrival, which is a lovely gesture and gives you an opportunity to get to know your visitors. We have never gone down this road, partly because we are lazy and partly because it would mean inviting them into our sitting-room at the start of the visit and this is an area we like to keep 'off limits' as far as possible. However, we do supply fresh milk on arrival so they can make their own beverages in their rooms, and we are aware guests aren't always feeling particularly sociable after a long, tiring journey.

You should offer to help guests with their luggage (those of you with bad backs will be glad to hear most decline). Either way guests should be escorted to their rooms, asked for registration details and given any simple instructions as appropriate for the establishment such as keys for window locks, whereabouts of spare blankets and pillows, breakfast arrangements, etc.

From the time of arrival our guests have free access to the house as the front door key is attached to the bedroom key. This has never presented us with a problem but there are some who think the house key should never be handed over and that hosts should arrange their schedule around the movements of their visitors. We do have two locks on our front door and only hand out the key to one so this provides some measure of protection.

You also have to remember that whilst a guest is staying in your home the bedroom is their room and only to be entered for essential purposes such as cleaning.

INFORMATION

Guests will find most of the information they need in the 'welcome' letter (see Figure 4) we leave in their room. Most ask about places to eat and having spent a lot of time putting crosses on visitors' maps, we now provide them with an annotated map showing the whereabouts of local eating houses, pubs and speciality restaurants. It is helpful to have collected menus from local eating establishments or at least have an idea of the cost of a meal and style of catering that can be expected. We resist making recommendations as it is difficult to judge what someone else might be looking for or what price they will be prepared to pay. We are also acutely aware that the quality, particularly in pubs, can be dependent on who is cooking on the night the guest visits.

We keep an up-to-date supply of timetables for trains and buses servicing the area and cards for local car hire and taxis. We have maps of the local area and London which visitors are welcome to borrow, together with a more comprehensive range of tourist information leaflets than that available in the bedroom folder. These are kept in the dining room so all guests have access.

HOUSEKEEPING

Guests often comment that the standards of hygiene and cleanliness are much higher in a B&B than in hotels. As one client put it, apart from first class establishments hotels are often 'a little grubby round the edges'. You may feel your bedrooms are hygienic but your customers may take a different view. We all have our benchmarks and as soon as I go into an unfamiliar bedroom where I will be sleeping I look at the state of the actual

The Farm House
Kent

Dear Mr and Mrs White

Welcome to our Farm House. We hope you have a comfortable stay and will find the following information helpful.

- **The Yale key** on your bedroom key ring is for the front door – turn clockwise to open.
- **Hot water**: Please run the tap for a while as the hot water can take a little while to come through.
- **TV channels**: BBC 1; BBC 2; ITV; Channel 4.
- **Evening meals**: There are several restaurants and pubs in the area – please ask for details.
- **Hospitality tray**: If you want replacements or fresh milk please ask.
- **An iron and board** are available on request.
- **Breakfast**: Served in the dining room, please let us know what time you would like it and any preferences, full English, etc (see Menu below).
- **Emergency**: In the event of an emergency overnight please knock on our bedroom door or ring the hand bell on the landing windowsill. If we are out use the telephone in the hall to call the service you want or 999.
- **Smoking**: You are welcome to smoke in the dining room at any time.

Please let us know if you need anything or you have any special dietary needs or wishes.

Yours sincerely

Breakfast menu

Orange juice/fresh fruit
—
Assorted cereals, yoghurt
—
Egg: fried, poached, boiled, scrambled
Bacon, sausage, tomato, mushrooms
—
Toast, croissant
—
Coffee or tea (English, Earl Grey or herbal)

(Twin or double £50, single £35 per night – inclusive of full breakfast)

Fig. 4. Sample welcome letter.

pillow and under-blanket. If these are spotless I then feel I can relax and trust the establishment to have kept everything else up to scratch, the sanitary ware having been properly disinfected and the tooth mug washed and dried in the kitchen, not rubbed round with the previous guest's hand towel. (You can tell I have had hotel experience!) Remember the fresh eye of a guest will often pick up what an owner has overlooked: smudges on windows, finger marks on light switches, dust round the edges of the carpet or under the bed.

I have found it helpful to create a housekeeping checklist – as much to save me from re-cleaning unnecessarily as to ensure everything is spotless. For instance it isn't necessary to clean the windows weekly whereas it is necessary to machine-wash the shower curtain very regularly.

The desire to meet high standards, such as a daily change of towels and linen, needs to be balanced with an environmental awareness to preserve water resources and conserve energy. Thus reusing of tablecloths and changing bed linen on alternate or every third day can be justified environmentally and also, fortunately, makes good business sense by increasing your margin of profit. Some proprietors choose to put this issue in their guests' court by placing a notice in their bathrooms offering clean towels but pointing out the environmental consequences. We change the bed linen every second or third day depending on the length of a guest's stay – ie we will change it once during a 4-day stay. The bathmats we change with each new let.

Housekeeping checklist

Following each let:

Bathroom
Remove dirty towels, bathmats, used soap, etc
Empty bin and remove tooth mugs for washing
Clean and disinfect WC
Thoroughly clean washbasin and bath, polish chrome
Wipe down shower curtain and change if necessary
Wipe down all surfaces
Clean tiles and windows if necessary
Put back clean towels and bath mats
Check toilet tissue, plus one extra
Replenish soap and toiletries
Replace clean tooth mugs
Wash floor with disinfectant
Survey room

Bedroom
Strip beds and remove dirty linen
Check under slips and mattress covers, machine wash frequently
Check blankets, bed covers and duvets for stains
Empty waste paper basket
Remove and replenish hostess tray
Make bed/s
Check inside of all drawers and wardrobes for left luggage and wipe
Wet clean/dust/polish all surfaces
Clean windows if necessary
Check carpet and walls for marks
Check lights, TV and electrical items
Vacuum clean floor
Survey room

A routine of care

Obviously rooms that are let need freshening up daily. Many (but not all) guests make their own beds and leave the room in immaculate condition so all that is required is to empty the waste paper basket, refill the hospitality tray and change the towels. When guests leave a thorough clean is necessary and I estimate it takes about an hour to service a double room. A routine is more essential than for your own family for it is surprising how spots on a mirror, dirty underwear in a bottom drawer or a teabag in the teapot can be overlooked if these are not checked after every guest.

It is in care over little things that the more individual approach of the B&B owner can score. If the day promises to be hot the windows and curtains can be closed to keep the room cool for later arrivals. In the winter the heating can be adjusted to the right level. A special touch, for both appearance and perfume, is a small vase of fresh flowers. And final check – do all the appliances, lights, heating and TV work?

MAINTENANCE

To maintain standards a number of activities need to be carried out on a regular basis. Mattresses should be turned, both end to end and side to side, probably once a month. Guests tend to perch on the side of the bed nearest the door and you will be surprised how this can wear down the springs. When staying in a self-catering flat recently I sat on the edge of the double bed and almost collapsed on to the floor, whereas the edge on the other side was comparatively firm – I was almost tempted to turn the mattress myself. When there are twin beds one often receives more wear than the other so it can be worthwhile changing the mattresses or beds over.

One area in which hotels often fail is marks on the carpet, nothing major, just drips from coffee cups and make-up. Regular spotting and shampooing make a great difference.

Extractor fans in bathrooms must be regularly checked for dirt and fluff – this was something we failed on at our last inspection. The grout between the bathroom tiles needs to be bleached regularly. Ceilings, walls and paintwork in the bedrooms and bathrooms will need to be redecorated every three years or so, with yearly touch-ups if the walls are emulsioned.

MEALS

Breakfast

It is as well to let guests know in advance any restrictions over the time this can be served. Some hosts prefer not to serve it before 7.30am which can be restrictive for business men, or after 9am, which might seem early to those who have been celebrating the night before.

The meal can be as simple or elaborate as you please but bear in mind what you are charging and whether it comes within your catering budget. Some providers take tremendous trouble to provide memorable breakfasts with homemade bread, muffins and all manner of cooked alternatives including kedgeree, smoked haddock and kippers. Whilst this is commendable it will put up the costs considerably and if you are charging a modest figure will leave little margin for profit. We consider the cost of breakfast should be no more than 15% of the per head price. We are not particularly adventurous mainly because 'full English' (or Irish, Scottish or Welsh), is what most guests ask for and we can have all the items on offer fresh.

We find it helps to ask for cooked orders when we ask the time guests wish to eat the night before. Speed can be of great importance to business people who usually have an early breakfast and like to be away within 15 minutes. To help us achieve this we have the sausages, bacon, tomato and mushrooms ready by the time they arrive at the table so only the eggs are cooked to order. If requested we can add or supplement baked beans, black pudding, fried bread and fried potatoes. If a guest particularly wanted smoked fish or kippers as an alternative we would oblige providing we had notice.

Breakfast options
Those who prefer a Continental style breakfast are likely to choose fruit juice, cereal, toast and coffee or tea. For those who want the full spread we provide cereal (muesli is the most popular), yoghurts and a bowl of fresh fruit. If asked, and particularly if guests stay for more than one night, we can supply fresh or tinned grapefruit, prunes, melon, fresh fruit salad or porridge. We offer locally made products where we can, sausages from the butcher in the village (though we have found many guests and particularly youngsters prefer a branded product), marmalade from the WI, croissants and bread from the local baker and our own eggs.

We choose to serve butter and preserves in dishes (scrupulously clean!) as we feel this is more in keeping with a home environment, but some hosts prefer one-portion packs of butter and preserves obtainable from a cash and carry which are of course totally hygienic. We offer a choice of English, Earl Grey or herbal tea or fresh coffee.

Loaves of brown and white bread are left in the dining room with a toaster so that visitors can make as much fresh toast as they like. This works well, apart from the smoke alarm going off as they fiddle with our carefully set dial – and we sometimes wonder whether they are familiar with a bread knife!

Other tips from our experience:

◆ Although most of us now have access to late opening shops we find it useful to keep a small back-up supply of breakfast basics in the deep freeze.

◆ We aim to keep cooking smells to a minimum as not everyone is in love with the smell of grilled bacon as they emerge from under the duvet.

◆ To serve breakfast we don matching aprons, much to the amusement of our friends.

◆ If we have guests eating alone we usually leave them our morning paper.

Evening meals
Unless these are offered as part of a home hospitality package this

will be very much a service rather than a source of income. If you are prepared to offer this extra service it needs to be made clear that you will need advance notice, the meal will be the cooking of the house and served at a set time.

OTHER SERVICES

You may have requests for packed lunches, storing luggage, and driving to and from airports and train stations. If you are happy to offer these additional services you will need to work out a scale of charges in advance.

SOCIALISING

We greet our guests by giving them our first name on meeting, and using theirs if they offer it. We are invariably surprised by the 'odd' relationship we have with our visitors. They pay us – then some tip us whilst others buy us small presents, kiss us goodbye or write letters of appreciation as though we were their friends not servants. Others prefer to maintain a distance and this you have to respect and adjust your own demeanour so as not to make the guest feel uncomfortable.

Overseas visitors appreciate the all-round experience of living in a family home and being able to sample the English way of life. Equally rewarding for us is to discuss their customs and views on life. A Dutch couple, on their first visit to the UK, told us how they had been dreading the reception they would receive having been told the English were distant and uncooperative. I'm pleased to say that together with the bar staff at our local pub we quickly dispelled this stereotype.

Breakfast tends to be the time for socialising, providing suggestions on local places of interest to visit, places to eat, the local transport system and geography of the country generally. Hence it is important that you should not be too pressed for time, but be aware there are the few who will linger over breakfast for hours and you will have to find a means to extricate yourself without causing offence.

COMPLAINTS

According to a VisitScotland tourism-training leaflet, '96% of dissatisfied customers don't complain but tell eight to ten people about their experience'. This does not surprise us. We have had very few unsolicited complaints since we started operating but this is not because we are wonderful, as I know from finding things that obviously weren't working such as the hot water system or the TV, after they have left! We used to have a rooster that provided the early morning call – any time from 4.30am depending on the time of year. Some visitors loved it – but I'm sure others hated it, and us as well, though they were more likely to walk with their feet than actually complain. I sometimes wonder whether it got mentioned on the postcards back home. Around this time I stopped asking people if they had slept well – if not I really didn't want to know.

Be prepared for the unexpected

You quickly learn never to be surprised when dealing with the public. We had a charming elderly Irishman booked in by our local TIC who was returning to his homeland having spent many years living and working in Australia. He arrived by taxi in slippers and with an assortment of cardboard boxes, and went to his bedroom for a shower and rest after his long journey. At 8pm we found him sitting quietly at the dining room table – waiting for breakfast. He was delighted with the boiled eggs we gave him and returned 12 hours later for his real breakfast.

Similarly, it is dangerous to assume anything. A couple of guests had the misfortune to be locked out by us. We had never met them as they arrived later than expected and we had made arrangements for them to pick up the key from a neighbour. When we arrived home late their car was in the drive and their room in darkness so we assumed they were safely tucked up in bed after a long journey. We put out all the lights, dropped the catch on the door and went to bed. Some while later I heard a jangling at the lock on the door and had to dash down to let them in. Arriving late after a long journey sitting in the car they had walked into the town for a late meal.

Guests may want to photograph your property, ours is pleasant but nothing exceptional but we have often seen cameras surreptitiously clicking in the garden or out of bedroom windows. More disconcerting is when they want to take a picture of the host and hostess and even the plate of 'full English'. We try to imagine the comments and laughter when they show these back home.

Taking note of needs

We cannot hope to be all things to all customers, but we try to be perceptive to their needs and because of the reluctance to complain watch for signs – what they leave on their plates; whether they help themselves to extra bedding. We also ask for feedback. Are you warm enough? Do you want to borrow an iron or use the washing machine? Any special food requests for breakfast? Incidentally according to the *Which Guide* the top complaint from B&B customers was 'the invisible host who appears only to hand over the key and receive payment'. Apparently a high percentage of complaints against operators relate to poor 'people' skills rather than the amenities. To help rectify this the courses, 'Welcome Host' and 'Welcome to Excellence' which are available through your local Tourist Board are to be recommended.

RULES

Trivial restrictions can be an irritation and we have found with the equitable relationship we enjoy with our visitors that none are necessary. Our guests have nearly all been extremely courteous and I think we enjoy the experience more by being flexible and having a relaxed attitude. We ask them what time they want breakfast; if they dither we suggest a time that suits us, usually 8.30am, and they invariably arrive 'on the dot'. When we first started hosting I used to lock the study and our bedroom door if we were out for the evening, but this is a habit I have long since dropped. We don't encourage guests to come into our sitting room or kitchen but have resisted the temptation to put 'private' on any of the doors.

However, your visitors' background and culture may be different from yours and not everyone understands the unwritten rules. Young people, whether staying because of work or leisure, can find the concept of staying in a private home where they are paying guests confusing. We have had guests helping themselves to the towels from our linen cupboard, using our bathroom although their rooms are en-suite and generally behaving as they would in their own homes. My husband was rather taken aback to find a teenage girl in her underwear putting on her make-up in front of the mirror in our bathroom – and she hadn't even thought to close the door!

We don't comment if guests bring in food to eat in their rooms as most do it very discreetly. But a few will order pizzas or Chinese takeaways that might not appeal because of the smell. When we get the opportunity we try to encourage them to use the dining room but most decline – and of course eating in the bedroom is what many families do in travel lodges.

Smoking

The anti-smoking lobby is strong and we are aware that some people find it a dirty, irritating habit and it can pose an insurance risk. In practice we have only had one detectable smoker in the bedroom in the past year but I must admit even when all the bedding had been washed and the furniture polished it took several days for the telltale smell to go. We do allow guests to smoke in the dining room, but most prefer to creep out into the garden. Whatever your policy it is imperative that the guests should be informed in advance so they can take the necessary action. We point out in our welcoming letter that smoking is permitted any time in the dining room.

CHILDREN AND YOUNG ADULTS

Children

It is your choice whether you choose to accommodate children but it is advisable to establish a clear policy to avoid misunderstandings. Children, although the responsibility of their parents, can present additional safety and privacy issues. We have found guests' youngsters rummaging in our kitchen cupboards and wandering around in the garage in search of toys, both places that contain potentially lethal items, so extra vigilance is necessary.

We don't have a minimum age policy as such and are happy to have children who can sleep in a room on their own (our rooms are adjacent). However, this is a form of preclusion as we usually charge the full rate for the child's room, which makes it an expensive option for families. We are happy to put a cot in either of the rooms but not an extra bed – even when a guest offers to bring their own. Our bedrooms really aren't big enough and we have found it is when there is insufficient room to move about freely that accidents happen. Because of possible crying we are also wary of letting one room to a couple with a baby when the other is occupied by a separate let.

Young adults

Experience has taught us that you have to be a bit bossy where young people are concerned, particularly if they are staying on a Saturday night following a wedding or party. They ask for a full breakfast at a certain hour but we find there is no movement and the curtains are tightly closed at the appointed time. Alternatively they appear for breakfast and then go back to bed! We have found it pays dividends to ask if they would like a call half an hour before breakfast. You will also need to close your eyes to very untidy rooms with the floor and bed acting as the wardrobe. I remember our own children as teenagers and try to see it as a positive – as I cannot get around the clutter to clean the room I needn't bother.

ANIMALS

Again the choice is yours but even if you love dogs remember many people don't and the real issue now is the increasing number of guests with allergy problems. The fact that we own a cat has been a deterrent to a few potential visitors and we had a charming American couple who wrote in our visitors' book that they would have come again had we not had a cat. As far as we know they never set eyes on the cat, which certainly never goes into the guest bedrooms, but she said she knew within ten minutes of being in the house there was one around and had to take appropriate medication.

It has been suggested that hosts should be proactive in informing intending visitors if they keep a pet, but it is our home and we feel it is up to them to ask the question and for animal lovers our cat is seen as a bonus. We don't usually accommodate dogs, though if we had a visitor with a guide dog we would, of course relent and one or two guests have been happy to leave their hounds in their cars. If you have the facilities to accept dogs and are happy with this it could be a good selling point as the facility is definitely in demand and the AA publish a guide of *Pet Friendly Places to Stay.*

DAMAGE TO FURNISHINGS

If you feel any damage cannot be accepted as fair 'wear and tear' you can add the cost of replacement to the guest's bill or send them a bill if the damage is discovered after their departure. Our shower fitment has been broken a couple of times and we have had a bedside light knocked on the floor and broken – as they were a pair we had to replace both. On each occasion our guests were very apologetic and we didn't ask for compensation.

DEPARTURE

This is as important as the welcome. We don't stipulate a time to leave, unless asked, but in practice most guests conform to an unspoken departure time around 10am. We offer to help with their luggage and both try to be available to shake hands and wish them a safe journey. We also take this opportunity to check that they have left the keys behind – our keys have been international travellers in the past.

REPEAT BUSINESS

This would seem to be the best guide for assessing customer satisfaction and may work if you are catering for business people, those making regular trips to the area or you provide specialist 'home hospitality'. We have never stayed at the same B&B twice, although this is no reflection on the standard of accommodation, simply that we take our vacations in different areas. Interestingly it is one area of business in which it would be possible to keep going even if nobody ever returns, unlike a shop or restaurant where it is important to build up a loyal clientele. Having said that you are unlikely to know who may return, so every guest should be treated as though they are a customer for life, and if they never come back they may recommend your establishment to their work colleagues, friends or family.

GUEST RECORDS

You can create as many records as you please to monitor your guests and there are software packages available to create occupancy charts and statistics.

The minimum requirements are:

◆ a diary to log reservations together with other relevant details taken at the time of booking;

◆ a guest register or registration form on which the legal requirements are recorded.

Some providers choose to transfer the information from the registration form to individual alphabetical card records with registration details and personal notes. This is a useful aide memoir which is easily accessed if the guest returns and can also be used for follow-up advertising.

LOOKING AFTER YOURSELF

Make life as easy as possible for yourself and your family. We have stayed in B&Bs where the owners have moved into a caravan in the garden for the 'season' so that they can get the maximum number of lets – fine as long as it doesn't cause too much strain within the family. If you don't want to be available 24/7 book in some time off. Maybe take guests Monday to Friday or long weekends only; close for certain weeks in the year and plan your own holidays well in advance so the dates are sacrosanct. A number of operators open for the main tourist season only and we are thinking we may restrict opening in the future to April to October.

You will need your privacy and should establish the limits in a friendly way as soon as possible, mainly by keeping doors shut or open according to whether guests are welcome.

Things can go wrong unexpectedly. It is very stressful if you double-book or are taken ill so you need to think through contingency plans. We have a good working relationship with other hosts in the area and have helped out with both these unforeseen events in the past. There have also been occasions when we have been able to warn each other about potential problem clients travelling in the area. Similarly encourage the goodwill of your neighbours and consult them from the outset to allay any fears. Ours have redirected lost travellers, helped out with handing over keys, sat in on our behalf waiting for guests to arrive, and on one occasion even took pity on a traveller who arrived late in the evening when we were away from home and gave him a bed for the night.

Filling Your Rooms 5

The extent to which you promote your B&B will depend on the level of occupancy you desire. If your principle motivation is the enjoyment you get from entertaining guests you may be fairly relaxed about the numbers who come through your door. If it is first and foremost a business venture you will want to seize every marketing opportunity. You also need to think about the type of customers you want to attract and how best to target them.

For those planning a move to buy a B&B business then location is likely to be your priority for enticing the most visitors. If, like us, you adapt your current home you will have to work within the available market and unless you have plenty of passing trade will need to advertise, particularly during off-peak periods.

If you are aiming mainly for the leisure market current trends in tourism will have an impact on your decision as to which areas to target. European visitors tend to operate on a tighter budget than holidaymakers from the States and this, together with the high rate of the £ in relation to other currencies, has meant that many overseas visitors, when they make it over here, have been favouring B&B in preference to more expensive options.

Statistics have established that the domestic market is most likely to be taking short breaks and not necessarily at weekends – retired clients often prefer to holiday mid-week as the tourist sites are quieter and with the flexibility in working patterns many workers are able to take time off during the week. In practice our main market has turned out to be couples aged 50+, a group we are very comfortable with and whom we would try to reach with any advertising campaign.

PROMOTIONAL LITERATURE

The majority of potential visitors will make their decision as to whether or not to make contact from what they see in your brochure, a printed guide book or on the internet, so illustrations and content need to be as appealing as you can make them.

A brochure, business card, or both are essential for responding to written and telephone enquiries, handing out to guests and distributing locally. You may choose to use the services of a graphic designer for professional artwork if your budget allows. I think it is a mistake to spend a great deal on a quality product or purchase large quantities of literature at the outset. We over-ordered a pricey brochure for a self-catering cottage 15 years ago and I'm still using the same brochure – with all its hand written annotations. Prices, in particular, are subject to change and if included these could make your brochure obsolete after one season.

Start by looking at the advertising brochures of others in the same field so you can identify what should be included and what makes a brochure special, then economise by using a home computer. We print our own leaflets using A4 card divided laterally into three. To this we attach a peel off coloured enprint or scanned-in photograph of the outside of the property and the accommodation grading sticker. These leaflets can be created and amended as the need arises and fit neatly into an A4 envelope.

We have kept the information simple using care not to breach the Trade Descriptions Act by overselling the virtues of our home and services. We also print our own business size card, with photo on back. Many proprietors design a more detailed folded brochure and include a location map and diagram of the accommodation.

FREE ADVERTISING

People who live and work locally will often be asked for accommodation recommendations so decide which clients you want to attract and then make use of free marketing opportunities. Think of anywhere with a possible need for overnight accommodation over a fairly wide catchment area and target them with your literature. Flyers and brochures can be left with local shops, pubs, offices, car rental companies, recognised tourist attractions, embassies, universities, boarding schools, research centres, estate agents and anywhere else that comes to mind locally.

SIGNING

For those who live on a main road an obvious and effective way of advertising is to put up a 'B&B' sign and in seasonal tourist areas travellers often rely on finding accommodation this way. This needs some thought. Consider how you would feel having strangers knocking on your door at 10.30pm looking for a room for the night. This is most likely to happen if they find they have had too much to drink to drive home and much more likely to occur if you display a sign. (You can, of course, turn them away but it could lead to an unpleasant encounter.) Additionally, if you live in a residential area a commercial sign is more likely to antagonise the neighbours and will probably be of little use anyway if there is no passing trade.

VISITBRITAIN, REGIONAL TOURIST BOARDS (RTB) AND TOURIST INFORMATION CENTRES (TIC)

The administration of tourism in Great Britain can be quite baffling to simple B&B providers. It devolves from VisitBritain, which is funded by the Department for Culture, Media and Sport, through the national and regional boards, district and county council initiatives, marketing consortiums and private enterprises. As one of our English guests remarked, 'It's easier for a Brit to book a holiday in Spain than in the UK'.

That said the RTB's marketing facilities, the local council tourism guides and TICs are the main resource we use to select accommodation when travelling around the country and we have found them to be our greatest friend as providers. Their promotion, either directly or indirectly, is the source of most of our custom whether tourists or business clients. They promote us through their guides, website and extensive advertising campaigns. They also provide an accommodation booking service claiming

10% commission on the first night's tariff. It is helpful to be proactive in working with your local TICs by phoning them when you have vacancies rather than waiting for them to contact you.

In addition to helping us let our accommodation the Tourist Boards are concerned with raising standards nationally so that visitors can have confidence in the quality they can expect. They do this by offering a National Quality Assurance Standards inspection scheme and providing opportunities to attend discounted training courses on such topics as food hygiene, customer care and a variety of computer courses. Apart from the 'compulsory' aspect if we wish the Tourist Board to promote us we have also found that being inspected under their scheme has given us greater confidence in the product we offer.

The downside of all this is that it costs money. You have to pay to be inspected and only then can you apply to advertise in the official brochures and guides. The fee you will be charged for inspection is subject to a 25% reduction if you are a Tourist Board member. Within the next few years it will become compulsory to have been inspected under the NQAS if you wish to participate in any form of advertising supported by public funds and long term this may become a legal requirement.

NATIONAL QUALITY ASSURANCE STANDARDS SCHEMES (NQAS)

There are three approved national bodies which carry out inspections: the AA, RAC and VisitBritain. All inspect to the same standards worked out on a points and percentage basis. Inspections cover a range of categories from self-catering to luxury hotels and were recently revamped so the emphasis is more on quality and the needs and expectations of visitors than facilities. For B&Bs, guest houses and inns the symbol in England is a diamond with a grading from 1 for the simplest to 5 at the luxury end. For the rest of Great Britain the symbol adopted is a star. As to what to expect for each rating I quote from the *Heart of Kent* guide.

◆ **One diamond** Clean accommodation; acceptable comfort with functional décor; comfortable bed with clean linen, towels and fresh soap; adequate heating and hot water for baths or showers; acceptable level of quality and helpful service.

◆◆ **Two diamonds** All the above and a sound level of quality and customer care in all areas.

◆◆◆ **Three diamonds** Good quality, comfortable bedrooms; well maintained practical décor; choice of quality items for breakfast; other meals if provided, freshly cooked with quality ingredients; good level of comfort and customer care.

◆◆◆◆ **Four diamonds** Very good level of quality in all areas; customer care showing very good levels of attention.

◆◆◆◆◆ **Five diamonds** Ample space with a degree of luxury; excellent quality beds, furniture, décor; breakfast – wide choice of high quality, fresh ingredients; other meals, if provided, featuring fresh, seasonal, local ingredients; excellent levels of customer care.

To these ratings gold and silver awards can be added for additional quality in the specific areas that guests identify as being really important for them.

We started with four diamonds and have since had a silver award added. Whilst we are happy with this we are also aware that it is better to exceed expectations and a higher grading may sometimes lead to customer dissatisfaction. Once accepted under the scheme you are committed to observing their code of conduct. In Northern Ireland you cannot legally set up in business until your visitor accommodation has been quality inspected.

THE INSPECTOR'S VISIT

The inspector can either book an unannounced overnight stay or have a prearranged day visit. In the event of a stay you will be paid the current overnight rate. Providers are given a comprehensive report of the assessment and everything will be taken into consideration from the tidy appearance of the hosts to the quality of the toilet tissue. We have found our inspectors helpful in giving positive suggestions as to how we should comply with our legal obligations, provide our guests with the greatest comfort, and save ourselves money. Other hosts have suggested their comments and recommendations are unnecessarily intrusive but I guess this is the price that has to be paid for standardisation. Initial approval is subject to an annual inspection.

Benefits of assessment
Those who meet the criteria:

◆ Have a free entry on the TIC's database throughout the UK and in over 40 countries abroad. There are currently more than 550 TICs across the country.

◆ Participate in a nationwide booking service.

◆ Are acceptable for inclusion in local authority regional guides – which are free to customers.

◆ Have a short free entry in the back of the only official British guide, the *Where to Stay Guide*. This is sold at bookshops throughout the UK.

◆ Have free listing on the VisitBritain internet sites.

◆ Can buy stickers and signs to display the logo and rating on promotional literature, websites and outside the property.

◆ Receive regular free updating newsletters.

◆ Have the opportunity to participate in an annual awards scheme.

◆ May attend courses run on behalf of the local Tourist Boards.

◆ Those with gold and silver awards are given the opportunity to appear in the promotional publication *Somewhere Special*.

We have found that our free advertising, together with the local TIC contacts and regional guide, have provided enough bookings for our needs, but if you are aiming for maximum occupancy or are situated in an area with less available business you will need to invest in other means to attract customers.

ACCOMMODATION GUIDE BOOKS

There are a range of guides; some supported by national organisations, some by local councils and others researched independently by their authors. The AA, RAC and VisitBritain each have their own annual guides for Quality Assurance inspected properties. These list the properties approved under this scheme but for a more detailed entry with illustration it is necessary to pay for an advertisement. These guides are then sold to the public at around £10 to £12.

Any entry in an annual guide book, for which the consumer pays, requires careful thought. You will need to establish the number of copies being printed and be clear as to why travellers might pay for a particular guide when there are complimentary ones fairly readily available. Once your address appears in the first publication you are likely to be swamped with requests to advertise in national, regional, county and local guides each offering their own websites, multi-lingual call centres and not-to-be-missed promises of promotion campaigns. Take care, this form of advertising is not cheap and there can be considerable overlap in coverage.

A plus is that visitors often use the same guide for several years but if this is a tentative venture you may come to regret the overexposure when you are still receiving phone calls and having folks knocking at the door years after you have given up or moved on. You can always change your phone number but it's not so easy to move the property!

Local authority regional guides
If you pick up a copy of the free holiday guide for your area from your nearest TIC, you will find it a colourful illustrated publication with maps and a comprehensive editorial on local attractions together with advertisements for hotels, guest houses, B&Bs and self-catering establishments that have been approved under their inspection scheme. In addition to the quality rating each property displays symbols indicating the facilities on offer such as languages spoken, evening meal, parking, dogs and/or children welcome. Any entry to the guide has to be submitted in the summer for printing in January, so you will need to decide prices and conditions six months in advance.

Commercial guides
Some private enterprise groups publish their own free holiday guides which look very similar to the local authority publications. Some, but not all, require advertisers to have been inspected under NQAS.

NETWORKING
If we cannot accommodate a potential guest we pass them on to others in the area, if we think they would appreciate the booking,

and they do the same for us. In some parts of the country hosts
have joined forces informally to promote their particular area.

Marketing consortia

Check if there are any marketing consortia you could join: farm
holidays, special interest holidays, local Bed and Breakfast
Associations, B&Bs of a particular quality. There are already a
number of such consortia that share the cost of advertising to
achieve the greatest coverage, many of which require inspection
under the Quality Assurance scheme for entry. The on-line
booking service many of these offer is particularly helpful to
overseas visitors.

Targeting particular interest groups

The 'grey pound' can be a remunerative source of income with
over a quarter of the population now over 55 and on the increase.
This sector of the public has the time to take leisure breaks, often
not too far from home, and many choose to combine this with a
particular hobby or interest. Depending on your location you
might consider advertising in specialist magazines, such as those
for bird watchers, anglers or art historians. Researching family
history is a popular hobby these days and some of the local
societies accept advertising in their quarterly magazines. If your
property has a memorable garden try magazines or guides that
specialise in this. If you offer a hospitality package and specialise
in quality catering try gourmet clubs and magazines. Some
national newspapers and magazines, such as the 'Sundays' and
The Lady promote the holiday industry.

INTERNET

This is fast becoming a popular means of seeking and booking accommodation and to own a computer and be connected to the internet is becoming an essential for even the smallest of businesses. VisitBritain maintains that one-third of British holiday makers use the internet to research and plan their holidays, and a recent winner of the 'B&B of the year' award registered with the AA attributed 80% of his business to this source.

Accommodation booking characteristics in 2002 for UK Residents[2]

	Millions
Firm booking via the internet	8.1
Firm booking made in person	8.7
Firm booking via telephone	44.3
Firm booking via e-mail	1.8
Firm booking via post	2.4

With improved search engines targeting potential customers has become a much less haphazard operation, and simply keying in the name of the nearest town or one of the regional Tourist Boards will enable interested customers to locate your personal entry on a tourist board or consortium site. Having discovered your entry it is essential that they should then be able to contact you quickly, if not by on-line booking at least by e-mail or phone. There is now sophisticated software, suitable for those running

---

[2] United Kingdom Tourism Survey (UKTS) 2002

B&Bs and guest houses, which enables proprietors to offer a complete reservation system over the internet. However, the statistics above indicate that the majority of potential guests still like to speak to their hosts before confirming a booking.

Tourist Boards are encouraging their members to go online to increase accommodation bookings and this is certainly an area that is destined to grow. As participants in their Quality Assurance inspection scheme we have free listing on the VisitEngland internet site but we have been slow to advertise our e-mail address as we feel we couldn't always respond quickly enough and have been warned by some hosts that they have found themselves in receipt of inappropriate, unwelcome e-mails.

Another disadvantage we foresee is that there is no way to screen a potential client. By having a conversation with a guest on the telephone you can at least pose questions to get a feel of whether you will be able to provide what they are looking for and they will suit you. However, our phone bookings are increasingly telling us that they first saw us on the internet and having our own website is something we will probably have to adopt within the next couple of years.

Websites

If you are a competent computer user you will probably be able to create your own website using one of the software programmes. As with your brochures check out other websites on the net and make yours as enticing and informative as possible so guests know exactly what to expect. Some Tourist Boards are offering reasonably priced courses for hosts who want to do their own desktop publishing and build their own websites, and if your site is put together with the help of others in the business you are more likely to establish the most appropriate links – a key requirement. The third alternative is to have your site created professionally, but this is likely to cost several hundred pounds.

SATURDAY NIGHT BOOKINGS

Making the best use of your available space to obtain maximum occupancy can be difficult. We learnt early on that it is necessary to work out a strategy for weekend bookings. It is too easy to fill up every Saturday night with local celebrations booked a long time in advance. These are fun, it being nice to be involved in local festivities, but they are not good business practice as they block beds for tourists who may want to stay two or three nights over a weekend.

We compromise by accepting a few weddings and restricting the period we will book to a month in advance. Incidentally wedding bookings are particularly prone to misunderstandings. If the bride, or her parents, book rooms you need to clarify exactly who will be occupying them. Young folks tend to change their minds, decide to sleep in the marquee or get a last minute offer of accommodation with friends and you are left with empty accommodation and not sure whom to pursue for the cost.

RETURN VISITS

To encourage repeat business you can remind past guests of your address and what you have to offer with Christmas cards or circular newsletters. Many of us are able to visualise exactly where we stayed but cannot remember either the address or name of the owners. Once you have been operating for a year or so you will have acquired a list of names and addresses – particularly useful to those offering hospitality packages.

Once up and running you can also carry out your own market survey. Ask every guest why he or she chose your area and then ended up on your doorstep, to give some guide as to the provenance of your clientele. Your chronological registration records will identify quiet periods and with this information you will be able to improve your marketing techniques and target your advertising.

Finally, if you really want to fill your rooms you must be available. A potential guest or TIC will only phone once and if they cannot make contact through a landline or mobile, they will move on to someone else. Some hosts choose to carry their mobiles all the time and others link up frequently to their answer machines. Care has to be taken with responding when away from home; first to ensure that you have a vacancy, which may mean carrying your business diary and secondly that nobody is accepting bookings on your landline at the same time – an all too easy way to double book. If you are to get bookings over the internet you will need to check several times a day.

" Do you accept payment in Danegeld? "

Money 6 *Matters*

PRICING

What should you charge? Not a very scientific formula but I think this is a combination of costs and what you can get away with. Relate your charges to expenses and overheads by costing out likely expenditure on laundry (check this out commercially, you may be in for a big surprise), cleaning equipment, food, heat and light, deterioration of furnishings, publicity and if appropriate the interest and capital return on any loan taken out to help you get established. Next get the local guides and check out what your competitors are charging; relevant factors to feed in will be location, diamond rating and additional facilities.

Plump for what you think the market will bear and then hope you will be left with enough to cover the cost of your labour and provide a small margin of profit. Those working for themselves are notorious for failing to cost in their time, and once in operation you will find it a useful exercise to log up the time you spend on activities such as cleaning, doing the laundry, laying up the breakfast table, cooking, serving and clearing breakfast.

When checking competitors' prices you may be surprised at the charges of some of the commercial establishments but remember they have to add 17½% VAT to their bills, and often run special offers which reduce their rack rates considerably. Hotels have to come up with ever-more attractive promotions to fill their rooms, such as 'Two nights for the price of one'. They need to do this during off peak periods as they have ongoing staff wages to pay and the hope is that they will recoup on extra restaurant meals and bar sales. Such gimmicks have limited appeal for B&B providers. They may improve your room occupancy statistics, possibly goodwill, but not your net profit.

Perhaps the greatest competition to B&B operators are the travel lodges and if there is one in your area you may wish to match or better their charges. However, as mentioned earlier there are potential problems with offering too competitive prices. These will appeal to overseas tourists who find the cost of living in the UK very high but can also be the first port of call for the destitute. When working with the Citizens Advice Bureau we used to hand out the tourist accommodation guide to the homeless as this was often the only available short-term option.

There are several options when fixing the price:

◆ Per guest or per room. We charge per room: £50 for a double or twin per night. This translates to £25 per person – not what we charge for a single.

- Offer a continental breakfast within the room price with extra for a cooked meal or offer a reduction for those who choose a continental breakfast.

- Depending on your location or type of business offer concessionary rates out of season.

- Offer reduced rates for stays of more than two or three days.

- Add a surcharge for one-night stays.

- For single occupancy of a double room: half the room rate; reduce the room rate price by 25%; add a single supplement to the per person price of £10 or so.

Single supplement

Single accommodation is a contentious issue as many people travel alone these days and invariably feel they get a bad deal. We started by offering single business travellers double rooms at half price but realised that as they simply add the entire cost of their accommodation to the bill they submit to their employers or clients this was not an area in which to be too generous. With this in mind we thought about the issue from our point of view – time spent cleaning the room and bathroom was more or less the same whether occupied by one or two people, and although there were savings on ingredients the same effort was needed to lay up and serve breakfast for one as for two. From the guest's point of view they have the advantage of a more spacious room. We have rationalised that we are entitled to charge more for single occupancy.

In some tourist areas it is almost impossible to obtain a single room in a B&B during the high season as providers persist in hanging out for a full double rate. We think this is short sighted as a single at $^3/_4$ rate for three nights, with only one breakfast to supply, is more beneficial than having the room empty for a night, and I know from experience how frustrating it can be trying to track down single accommodation with en-suite facilities. We feel we are justified in asking for a supplement on the per person rate, in our case of £10, but as with all these issues supply and demand will probably dictate your decision.

We sometimes make concessions for stays of more than two nights as, generally speaking, when guests are in residence their rooms need little attention apart from emptying the waste paper basket and washing up the crockery on the hostess tray. Some hosts approach this from a different viewpoint and either will not take one-night bookings or add a surcharge for those staying only one night. We have often found tourists will book for just one night and then choose to stay for two or three more. We always congratulate ourselves when this happens!

Rates for children

Charging for children is another issue that needs addressing. We charge nothing for babies and as any children have to occupy a separate room we charge the rate for the room with a small reduction on the cost of breakfast. Those with family rooms, or where an extra bed is put up in a parent's room, usually add a supplement to cover the cost of food and laundry such as a standard £10 or an amount adjusted according to age, e.g. £8 for an 8-year old.

Something we find particularly galling is the amount our guests will spend on their evening meals. We tend to assume they are on a budget because they choose B&B and then find they spend on one meal the cost of two nights with us including full breakfasts! It would seem accommodation providers might be undervaluing their services.

DISPLAYING CHARGES

The Consumer Protection Act makes it an offence to give misleading information on prices and as customers like to know in advance what they are going to spend it is good practice to make this clear from the outset. Our charges appear in the local guide, on our brochures and on the information we leave in the rooms. In Northern Ireland and Scotland accommodation providers, irrespective of size, must display the scale of charges for accommodation and services in the entrance hall or reception area. As prices that appear in publications have to be decided at least six months in advance using the option of quoting 'from...' gives some leeway if you have pitched it too low, but makes it doubly important to clarify the price with each booking.

FRIENDS AND NEIGHBOURS

It is always a dilemma when friends, neighbours and acquaintances ask you to accommodate their visitors – should you charge and if so how much? We try not to operate two tariffs and ask ourselves the question, 'Would they have asked us or would we have offered if we didn't do B&B?' If the answer is 'no' we charge the standard rate.

RECEIPT OF PAYMENT

Luxury B&Bs present their guests with bills on headed paper that also serves for advertising. We use a numbered, duplicate cash receipt book plus sticker with our name and address. We also take the opportunity to add a small visiting card should they wish to come again. Bills are usually presented at breakfast on the last morning but sometimes guests ask to pay in advance – a proposition we are always happy to accept.

We accept sterling cheques and cash including euros. We did once, in ignorance, take a German cheque and rued the day, as the bank charges were so high. We don't as yet take credit cards, as we are familiar with our clientele and at present do not think it is necessary to pay for this facility. However, we have an open mind and may change in the future, particularly if we found we were doing more commercial business. One advantage of accepting credit/charge cards is that you can take a deposit on the phone and, providing it is made clear and agreed by the guest, you can claim in the event of a cancellation. We feel, however, that this would be rather high handed for our informal and friendly type of business and is more in keeping with a guest house or hotel.

We have noticed a growing trend for B&B prepaid vouchers purchased in the tourist's country of origin. We used this system in America many years ago and it seems to work well in Ireland. However, guests who cannot find B&Bs who are in the system able or willing to take them have highlighted potential problems. It seems to be that as the vouchers are discounted hosts on the list are reluctant to take them at busy times when there is no difficulty in letting at full price.

BUDGETING

As with all self-employment your income will be sporadic which might mean you need to monitor cash flow carefully.

Forecasting the future is not easy but a necessary part of business planning. Estimating income will be difficult until you have completed at least one full year. Some providers will have a steady flow of visitors whereas others will find considerable fluctuations according to season.

It is easier to anticipate costs (see Figure 5), which need to be broken down into fixed and variable. Fixed costs have to be paid throughout the year irrespective of the level of business. They include a proportion of water and sewerage rates, insurance, interest on loans (if applicable), publicity, Tourist Board membership and depreciation of furniture and fittings. It is advisable to discuss with your tax office the proportion of fixed costs that can be allocated. Variable costs include heat and light, food and drink, cleaning materials and laundry, stationery and postage.

FINANCIAL RECORDS

We are all required by law to keep records for tax purposes and if you are a limited company (not very likely) you will need to keep audited accounts. There are standard account books and computer programmes available for this purpose, or you may prefer to use the services of an accountant, particularly if you have

Item	Details	£
Food		
Housekeeping supplies		
Laundry		
Maintenance		
Heat and light		
Water and sewerage		
Postage and stationery		
Insurance		
Advertising		
Telephone and internet		
Travel		

Fig. 5. Estimated monthly costs.

more than one business. Those without bookkeeping experience
might also consider seeking the assistance of a professional at
least at the time of setting up. The bookkeeping system you
choose can be as simple or sophisticated as you like but the
minimum you will need is a dedicated bank account and an
income and expenditure account to record receipts and payments.

Bank account

First and foremost it is essential to keep your business income
and expenditure separate from your personal finances. By setting
up a separate private bank account you will be putting in place
the centre of your financial operation, with the bank statements
confirming your records. All income will be paid into this account
and all variable B&B expenses, together with a cheque for petty
cash for small items, paid out.

Income and expenditure account

To satisfy the Inland Revenue and for your own interest you will
need accurate records. This means keeping copies of *all* receipts,
apportionment of household bills relevant to the business, and
maintaining a comprehensive accounting system. To simplify the
accounts it is advisable to buy separately for the B&B otherwise
you will be forever extracting individual items from your shopping
receipts.

An income and expenditure account, cross-referenced with the
bank statement, will ensure you keep tabs on all your receipts and
payments (see Figure 6). As it is likely all income will be from the
same source a single column will suffice with the information
taken from the cash receipt book. The expenses side will need to

Income

		Total	Food	Laundry/ cleaning	Sundries	Utilities apportioned	Maintenance	Total	Profit/loss
									(Expenditure)
May 03		£	£	£	£	£	£	£	£
Wk 1	B&B sales	320	48	9	12	12	0	157	163
Wk 2	"	400	56	12	18	15	0	184	216
Jan 04		£	£	£	£	£	£	£	£
Wk 1	B&B sales	0	0	0	12	10	80	112	−112
Wk 2	"	100	10	5	15	12	120	182	−82

Gross profit in May – positive cash flow
Loss in January – negative cash flow

Food	= breakfast/sundry food items
Laundry/cleaning	= washing and cleaning materials/bathroom supplies
Sundries	= stationery/telephone/advertising/travel
Apportioned items	= gas/electricity/insurance
Maintenance	= repairs/decoration/replacements

Fig. 6. Example of a simple weekly income and expenditure account.

be itemised into columns, for food, cleaning materials, utilities, sundries, etc (similar to the estimated monthly costs). By reconciling your accounts, at least monthly, it is less likely that you will lose track of your income and expenses and it will be a reminder not to take more out of the business than it is making.

TAXATION

VAT

Liability for Value Added Tax depends on annual turnover. The current (2004/5) threshold for VAT is £58,000. Guest house operators may have to consider this but it is unlikely that with six guests or less you will reach this level unless the quality of accommodation and service is so high that you can charge a premium price per head. Another scenario is if you also run other businesses, then the combined turnover may put you over the limit. If you can avoid VAT it would certainly be helpful as it would mean an increase of 17½% on your prices and although you could claim on expenses this would be small as food is zero-rated. If in any doubt ask your accountant or contact the local Customs and Excise VAT Office.

Income tax

Income from B&B is looked upon as self-employment for tax purposes. If your annual turnover is more than £15,000 or you have other sources of income such as businesses, investments and pensions it will be best to discuss your situation with an accountant. With a turnover under £15,000 you have two options – either to complete the self-employment form in the normal way or take advantage of the more straightforward Rent-a-Room exemption scheme. To clarify which option best suits your situation you should contact your local tax office and obtain the appropriate help sheets.

Self-employment

Those who follow this route of 'gross takings minus expenses' for tax purposes need to take careful note of what are allowable business expenses. Generally speaking these are costs incurred solely for the purpose of earning business profits and will include not only food and cleaning materials but also a proportion of other outgoings related to the parts of your home used exclusively for B&B, such as electricity, insurance and use of the car for B&B purposes – say one trip a week.

National Insurance

The self-employed, under state retirement age, are required by law to pay Class 2 National Insurance contributions even if it is just a spare time occupation and they are paying Class 1 contributions as well. The current rate is £2 per week. You can apply for a small earnings exception if your income from self-employment is below the £4,095 threshold.

RENT-A-ROOM FOR TRADERS

This is a simpler alternative for the 'hobby' operator. Under this system the first £4,250 of income (known as Rent-a-Room relief) will be exempt from income tax. Any income above this figure will be liable for tax and expenses will not be deductible. Bearing in mind that this requires the minimum of paper work you may find it the preferred option but it is a must that you declare and keep accurate paper work in support of all income. Additionally the gross receipts over the exemption limit are treated as taxable rental income instead of actual profits which can work to your advantage.

If the business is the declared occupation of one person only, and this is their only source of income, they will qualify for a personal allowance of £4,745 or £6,830 if over 65 (2004/5). So if the gross income for the year was £10,000 you can deduct the £4,250 Rent-a-Room relief and then qualify for a £4,745/£6,830 personal allowance. Whichever option you choose there is a wide range of leaflets available from any Inland Revenue Enquiry Centre or Tax Office.

As we use this option to pay our tax we do not need a detailed record of expenses, though we do need to keep track of payments for business purposes. Having kept detailed accounts for the first few years we have worked out the cost of breakfast and servicing the room on a per head basis. This we use to pay out disbursements rather than itemising all the household bills. This keeps paper work to the minimum.

Be warned that B&B operators, along with other self-employed categories, are often targeted for not disclosing all their income or deducting personal expenses as business expenses. The Tax Office has targeted hosts in the area where we live in recent years.

From B&B to Guest House

7

If providing serviced accommodation is to be your sole means of livelihood you will almost certainly need a larger establishment than a B&B with three letting bedrooms. You will find once you start hosting more than six guests that your property will change from being a home first and business second to the other way round. Indeed, depending on the number of bedrooms and range of services offered, you could be getting into the realms of hotel and catering management and it would be helpful, if not essential, to have had some training or education in the industry. Whether buying an existing business as a going concern, or adapting a property, you will certainly be looking at a more complex venture; maybe a restaurant which provides meals other than breakfast; possibly a licensed bar and almost certainly you will be looking at employing staff.

With the change to a more commercial enterprise the recommendations for a small B&B will still apply but with added responsibilities, and because of the additional legal requirements and financial risks you will almost certainly need the services of a solicitor and financial adviser before you venture forth. *Buying and Running a Guesthouse or Small Hotel* by Dan Marshall, published by How To Books, will be a very helpful starting point.

To give you some insight here are a few of the issues you may have to address.

LEGAL AND FINANCIAL

◆ What effect running a business will have on your personal finances.

◆ Whether to remain a sole trader or become a partnership or limited company.

◆ If it is a new business planning permission and 'change of use' will be necessary.

◆ It will be an offence to use the premises without a fire certificate. Under the Fire Precautions Act 1971, hotels and guest houses need to obtain a fire certificate if the property can take more than six people at one time. To qualify for a fire certificate you will need to supply and maintain fire blankets, fire extinguishers, smoke alarms and maybe fit fire doors and escapes.

◆ The house will now be a non-domestic property so you will have to pay business rates, which will also have capital gains tax implications when you sell the property.

◆ You may need to register for VAT, which could increase your prices by up to 17½%.

◆ You will have to pay an increased fee for a television licence if there are more than 15 rooms.

◆ You are more likely to employ staff so employment law will have to be followed, e.g. compiling a written Health and Safety policy and display a poster; complying with the national minimum wage, working time regulations, annual paid leave, parental leave, etc.

◆ Signage for the property will need to be more obvious, such as illuminated signs or signs approaching the property – which require planning permission.

◆ Prices will have to be displayed prominently.

◆ You are more likely to hold personal details of guests on a computer so you will need to notify the Data Protection Commissioner.

◆ You may wish to sell alcoholic drinks so will need a licence. Even if it is just a residential licence this entails a complicated application procedure and additional regulations regarding hours, children, etc.

OPERATING A GUEST HOUSE

◆ You will need to advertise more to fill rooms and have a website, preferably with on-line booking.

◆ The booking system will need to be more formal to keep track of reservations.

◆ More services are likely to be offered, such as evening meals and possibly a licensed bar which will probably require staff.

◆ The time factor may mean out-sourcing laundry.

◆ You will probably need to accept credit cards which will mean additional costs.

Summary

There is a lot of interest in running a B&B, as we are aware from the probing questions put to us by guests, friends and acquaintances. As a potential host you need to start by analysing why you want to do this – is it mainly for a lifestyle change or the money you hope to earn? Will you take all comers to create the highest room occupancy or will you gear your quality and prices to a specific type of clientele, who may or may not be forthcoming? Depending on what you hope to get out of it will determine the type of establishment you run; the market you will be aiming for; what you should buy or how you should adapt your present property and how you will decorate, furnish and equip it.

Having established your objectives think about the steps you can take to make it successful, then keep abreast of changes in the market, for instance the number of visitors from the USA has fallen (down by 10% on 2002) whereas that from Europe has increased, all of which has a bearing on advertising.

We have been asked on several occasions, 'What is the worst thing about doing B&B?' I can honestly say there is nothing that particularly bugs us. A long run of early mornings can be a bit wearing for the cook and a succession of 'one-nighters' can frustrate the housekeeper, but nothing is for ever.

SHARING YOUR HOME

Whatever your reasons or however you choose to operate your business you will be giving guests, and particularly visitors from overseas, an insight into both your home and locality in a way in which no one else can, so you have to offer a genuinely warm welcome.

Much of the official advice you will be obliged, or recommended, to follow relates to standardisation of facilities and service (dare I say bureaucracy) but remember your home is unique and should stay that way. Resist the temptation to adopt the latest styles in décor or furnishings – you can still run a professional operation without having to conform to what is perceived as the ideal package. In our opinion it's the individuality of each B&B and the care it can provide for its visitors that is its main attraction and is why guests will remember you long after they have forgotten the local travel lodge.

Sharing our home with strangers has enriched our life; every guest is a different challenge and every satisfied customer a cause for a pat on the back. Whilst it is easy to start off with enthusiasm it is equally important to maintain your original standards. Once you find yourself cutting corners it is probably time to rethink whether this is really what you want to do.

Further Information

USEFUL PUBLICATIONS

The Pink Booklet 4th edition (2000), English Tourist Board (VisitBritain). A practical guide to legislation for accommodation providers, obtainable with other information regarding setting up in business in an advice pack from your Regional Tourist Office.

Caterer and Hotelkeeper Weekly trade magazine, useful for estate agents specialising in serviced accommodation and suppliers of commercial equipment. From any newsagent.

Bed and Breakfast News An independent monthly newsletter obtainable from Regent House, Bexton Lane, Knutsford WA16 9AB.

Annual guides

Where to Stay: Bed and Breakfast Guest Accommodation. Official VisitBritain Guide.

Where to Stay: Somewhere Special. Official VisitBritain Guide.

The Bed & Breakfast Guide – England, Scotland, Wales, Ireland, Channel Islands. AA.

Hotels and Bed & Breakfast. RAC.

Scotland: Where to Stay – Bed & Breakfast. Scottish Tourist Board quality assessed properties.

Alastair Sawday's Special Places to Stay – British Bed & Breakfast. Alastair Sawday Publishing.

Alastair Sawday's Special Places to Stay – Bed & Breakfast for Garden Lovers. Alastair Sawday Publishing.

Bed & Breakfast Stops. FHG publications.

England, Wales & Scotland Charming Bed & Breakfast. Karen Brown's Guides.

The Best Bed & Breakfast, England, Scotland, Wales. Mortimer, Welles and Darbey.

COURSES

There are a number of training courses available to the UK tourism industry including:

◆ first aid;

◆ basic, intermediate and advanced food handling courses to encourage best practice;

◆ Welcome Host – a one-day training programme which concentrates on improving customer care skills.

◆ Welcome to Excellence – customer training for the tourism industry which aims to improve standards in customer care.

Advice and information on these can be obtained from the Regional Tourist Boards and local further education colleges.

USEFUL WEBSITES

Promoting Great Britain
www.visitbritain.com

England
www.visitengland.com
(to be EnglandNet in the future)

Ireland
www.visitireland.com www.nitn.com
www.discovernorthernireland.com
www.visittourismireland.com
www.discovernorthernireland.com

Scotland
www.visitscotland.com

Wales
www.visitwales.com

Consortia and agents
www.specialplacestostay.com
www.farmstayuk.co.uk
www.nifcha.com
www.bedandbreakfastnationwide.com
www.visitus.co.uk
www.wolsey-lodges.co.uk

Government bodies
www.inlandrevenue.gov.uk
www.dataprotection.gov.uk

Disability
www.holidaycare.org.uk
www.disability.gov.uk

USEFUL ADDRESSES

General
Data Protection Commissioner's Office
Wycliffe House
Water Lane
Wilmslow SK9 5AF
Tel: 01625 545745
E-mail: mail@notification.demon.co.uk
Website: www.dataprotection.gov.uk

Disability
Holiday Care
2nd Floor, Imperial Buildings
Victoria Rd
Horley
Surrey RH6 7PZ
Tel: 01293 774535
E-mail: holiday.care@virgin.net
Website: www.holidaycare.org.uk

Quality assessment
AA Contact Centre
Carr Ellison House
William Armstrong Drive
Newcastle-upon-Tyne
NE4 7YA
Tel: 0870 600 0371
Website: www.theAA.com

RAC Hotel Services
RAC House
1 Forest Rd
Feltham
Middx TW13 7RR
Tel: 020 8917 2840
E-mail: hotelservices@rac.co.uk
Website: www.rac.co.uk/hotels

Consortiums
Farm Stay UK Ltd
National Agricultural Centre
Stoneleigh Park
Warwickshire CV8 2LG
Tel: 024 7669 6909
E-mail: enquiries@farmstayUK.co.uk
Website: www.farmstayuk.co.uk

Town and Country Homes Association Ltd
Belleek Road

Ballyshannon
Co. Donegal
Tel: 00353 71 98 22222
Fax: 00353 71 98 22207
E-mail: admin@townandcountry.ie
Web: www.townandcountry.ie

Scotland's Best B&Bs
Clach Mhuilinn
7 Harris Road
Inverness IV2 3LS
Tel: 01463 242 092
E-mail: jacqui@ness.co.uk

Scottish Farmhouse Holidays
Lisa Wilson
Renton Terrace
Eyemouth
Berwickshire TD14 5DF
Tel: 01890 751 830
E-mail: scotfarmhols@compuserve.com

Wolsey Lodges
9 Market Place
Hadleigh
Ipswich
Suffolk IP7 5DL
Tel: 44 (0) 1473 822058
Fax: 44 (0) 1473 827444
E-mail: info@wolsey-lodges.co.uk

NATIONAL AND REGIONAL TOURIST BOARDS

VisitBritain
Thames Tower
Black's Road
London W6 9EL
Tel: 0181 846 9000
Fax: 0181 563 0302
Website: www.visitbritain.com

VisitEngland
Thames Tower
Black's Road
London W6 9EL
Tel: 0181 846 9000
Fax: 0181 563 0302
Website: www.visitengland.com

VisitScotland
Thistle House
Beechwood Park North
Inverness IV2 3ED
E-mail: tom.buncle@stb.gov.uk
Website: www.holiday.scotland.net

VisitScotland (Edinburgh)
23 Ravelston Terrace
Edinburgh EH4 3TP
Tel: 0131 332 2433

Scotland – Area Tourist Boards
Aberdeen and Grampian Tourist Board
Tel: 01224 288800

Angus and Dundee Tourist Board
Tel: 01382 527 549

Argyll, the Isles, Loch Lomond, Stirling and Trossachs Tourist
Board
Tel: 01786 445 222

Ayrshire and Arran Tourist Board
Tel: 01292 678 100

Dumfries and Galloway Tourist Board
Tel: 01387 245 550

Edinburgh and Lothians Tourist Board
Tel: 0131 473 3600

Greater Glasgow and Clyde Valley Tourist Board
Tel: 0141 204 4480

The Highlands of Scotland Tourist Board
Tel: 01977 421 1160

Kingdom of Fife Tourist Board
Tel: 01592 750 066

Orkney Tourist Board
Tel: 01856 872 001

Perthshire Tourist Board
Tel: 01738 627 958

Scottish Borders Tourist Board
Tel: 01750 20555

Shetland Islands Tourism
Tel: 01595 693 434

Western Isles Tourist Board
Tel: 01851 701 818

Wales Tourist Board
Brunel House
2 Fitzalan Road
Cardiff CF24 OUY
Tel: 029 20499909
E-mail: info@tourism.wales.gov.uk
Website: www.visitwales.com

Northern Ireland Tourist Board
St Anne's Court
59 North St
Belfast BT1 1NB
Tel: 028 9023 1221
Fax: 028 9024 0960
E-mail: info@nitb.com
Website: www.discovernorthernireland.com

Guernsey Tourism
PO Box 23
St Peter Port
Guernsey GY1 3AN
Tel: 01481 726 611
Fax: 01481 721 246
E-mail: enquiries@guernseytouristboard.com
Website: www.guernseytouristboard.com
(Guernsey, Sark, Alderney, Herm, Lithou and other smaller islands)

Isle of Man Tourism
Department of Tourism and Leisure
Sea Terminal Buildings
Douglas
Isle of Man IM1 2RG
Tel: 01624 686 801
Fax: 01624 686 800
E-mail: tourism@gov.im
Website: www.visitisleofman.com

Jersey Tourism
Liberation Square
St Helier
Jersey JE1 1BB
Tel: 01534 500 700
Fax: 01534 500 899
E-mail: info@jersey.com
Website: www.jersey.com

England's Regional Tourist Boards
Cumbria Tourist Board
Ashleigh
Holly Road
Windermere
Cumbria LA23 2AQ
Tel: 01539 444 444
Fax: 01539 444 041
E-mail: info@golakes.co.uk
Website: www.golakes.co.uk

East of England Tourist Board
Toppesfield Hall
Hadleigh
Suffolk IP7 5DN
Tel: 01473 822 922
Fax: 01473 823 063
E-mail: eastofenglandtouristboard@compuserve.com
Website: www.eastofenglandtouristboard.com
(Bedfordshire, Cambridgeshire, Essex, Hertfordshire, Norfolk, Suffolk)

North West Tourist Board
Swan House
Swan Meadow Road
Wigan Pier
Wigan WN3 5BB
Tel: 01942 821 222
Fax: 01942 821 002
E-mail: info@nwtb.org.uk
Website: www.nwtourism.net
(Lancashire, Greater Manchester, Cheshire, Derbyshire Peak
District and Liverpool with Merseyside)

Northumbria Tourist Board
Aykley Heads
Durham City
Durham DH1 5UX
Tel: 0191 375 3000
Fax: 0191 386 0899
E-mail: enquiries@ntb.org.uk
Website: www.e-northumbria.net
(Tees Valley, County Durham, Northumberland, and Tyne and
Wear)

South West Tourism
Woodwater Park
Rydon Lane
Exeter EX2 5WT
Tel: 0870 442 0830
Fax: 0870 442 0840

E-mail: post@swtourism.co.uk

Website: www.swtourism.co.uk

(Bath, Bristol, Cornwall, Isles of Scilly, Devon, Dorset, Somerset and Wiltshire)

Tourism South East – East

The Old Brew House

Warwick Park

Tunbridge Wells

Kent TN2 5TU

Tel: 01892 540766

Fax: 01892 511008

E-mail: enquiries@seetb.org.uk

Website: www.tourismsoutheast.com

(East and West Sussex, Kent and Surrey)

Tourism South East – West

40 Chamberlayne Road

Eastleigh

Hampshire SO5 5JH

Tel: 02380 625 400

Fax: 02380 620 010

E-mail: info@southerntb.co.uk

Website: www.southerntb.co.uk

(Berkshire, Buckinghamshire, Hampshire, Isle of Wight, Oxfordshire)

Visit Heart of England
Woodside
Larkhill Road
Worcester WR5 2EZ
Tel: 01905 761 100
Fax: 01905 763 450
E-mail: info@hetb.co.uk
Website: www.hetb.co.uk
(Derbyshire, Gloucestershire, Herefordshire, Leicestershire, Northamptonshire, Nottinghamshire, Oxfordshire, Cotswolds, Rutland, Shropshire, Staffordshire, Warwickshire, West Midlands, Worcestershire, Lincolnshire)

Yorkshire Tourist Board
312 Tadcaster Road
York YO2 2HY
Tel: 01904 707 961
Fax: 01904 701 414
E-mail: info@ytb.org.uk
Website: www.yorkshiretouristboard.net
(East Riding of Yorkshire, North, South and West Yorkshire, North East and North Lincolnshire)

Visit London Business and Conventions
1 Warwick Row
Victoria
London SW1E 5ER
Tel: 020 7932 2000
Fax: 020 7932 0222

E-mail: enquiries@londontouristboard.co.uk
Website: www.londontouristboard.com
(Greater London)

Index

If you want to know how...

- To buy a home in the sun, and let it out
- To move overseas, and work well with the people who live there
- To get the job you want, in the career you like
- To plan a wedding, and make the Best Man's speech
- To build your own home, or manage a conversion
- To buy and sell houses, and make money from doing so
- To gain new skills and learning, at a later time in life
- To empower yourself, and improve your lifestyle
- To start your own business, and run it profitably
- To prepare for your retirement, and generate a pension
- To improve your English, or write a PhD
- To be a more effective manager, and a good communicator
- To write a book, and get it published

If you want to know how to do all these things and much, much more...

howtobooks

If you want to know how...to become self-employed

Many people would perhaps like to be self-employed, but have never experienced life outside of a nine-to-five job. By the end of reading this book, you should have some idea of what the world of the self-employed is like.

John Whiteley

Going for Self-Employment
How to set up and run your own business
JOHN WHITELEY

The essential guide for anybody who wants to set up a business. It spells out the pros and cons of self-employment; assesses the risks involved; and offers solutions to raising finance, managing resources and complying with regulations. There's also useful advice on getting customers, dealing with book-keeping, administration and how to get ahead of your competitors.

ISBN 1 85703 920 3

If you want to know how...to enjoy an enriching retirement

When you retire you'll have 45–50 hours a week of extra free time. Even the most absorbing hobbies and interests are unlikely to fill that gap. If a job is what gave you your life structure, you'll need to replace that structure in retirement. Your happiness depends on understanding your own needs and structuring both time and activity to meet those needs.

Your Retirement Masterplan
How to ensure you have a fulfilling and enjoyable third age.
JIM GREEN

This book shows you how to turn retirement into a new lease of life. You'll find tried and tested templates which you can adjust according to your own inclinations and needs to produce a master plan for a successful and rewarding journey into the third age.

ISBN 1 85703 987 4

If you want to know how...to run a successful small business

'Running a business is never easy. More often than not it's a roller-coaster ride through a range of hazards and difficulties. But one thing is for sure: life will rarely, if ever, be dull. This book has one single purpose – to help you build a better business.'

Neil Bromage

100 Ways To Make Your Business A Success
A resource book for small businesses
NEIL BROMAGE

"Avoid those pitfalls and hit big time." – *Sunday Mail*

"No waffle, no preaching, just straightforward advice written in an unfussy, no bulls..t manner. What a nice change." – K. Trimble, Gaelkat Ltd

"The book is a valuable source of factual information that can be utilised in local and nationwide businesses." – The Gazette

ISBN 1 84528 017 2

If you want to know how...to do your own book-keeping and accounting

'In "doing the books" you will be at the very heart of the business, with your hands on the controls. You will be involved in the management of its assets and liabilities, its expenses and its profit margins.'

Peter Taylor

Book-keeping & Accounting for the Small Business
How to keep the books and maintain financial control over your business
PETER TAYLOR

'A guide to accounting procedures for sole traders, partnerships and limited companies... includes real life examples' – The Times

'Compulsory reading for those starting a new business and for those already in the early stages.' – Manager, National Westminster Bank (Midlands)

'An easy-to-understand manual on double-entry book-keeping that anyone can follow.' – Business First

ISBN 1 85703 878 9

If you want to know how...to prepare a business plan

'Preparing a business plan is crucial to help ensure the success of your business. A well researched and carefully structured business plan is the single most important component in the development and continuation of any venture.'

Matthew Record

Preparing a Winning Business Plan
How to win the attention of investors & stakeholders
Matthew Record

"This book will not only help you prepare a business plan but will also provide a basic understanding of how to start up a business." – Working from Home

"An excellent reference for even the most inexperienced business person looking to march into the business world ably armed with a professional plan." – Home Business Alliance

ISBN 1 85703 881 9

If you want to know how...to get free publicity

If your company, club, church or charity has a story to tell or something new, free or amazing to offer, journalists want to hear from you.

Getting Free Publicity
Secrets of Successful press relations
PAM AND BOB AUSTIN

This step-by-step manual takes you right through from who you should target and what journalists are looking for, to practical suggestions for choosing and presenting stories that will get accepted by editors. You will discover how to write effective press releases and articles, how to deal with media interviews and what to do if a journalist gets your story wrong.

ISBN 1 85703 972 6

How To Books are available through all good bookshops, or you can order direct from us through Grantham Book Services.

Tel: +44 (0)1476 541080
Fax: +44 (0)1476 541061
Email: orders@gbs.tbs-ltd.co.uk

Or via our website

www.howtobooks.co.uk

To order via any of these methods please quote the title(s) of the book(s) and your credit card number together with its expiry date. For further information about our books and catalogue, please contact:

How To Books
3 Newtec Place
Magdalen Road
Oxford OX4 1RE

Visit our web site at

www.howtobooks.co.uk

Or you can contact us by email at info@howtobooks.co.uk